745

AMAZING MODELS!
RUBBER BAND POWER

PETER HOLLAND

03821

ARGUS BOOKS

ARGUS BOOKS
ARGUS HOUSE
BOUNDARY WAY
HEMEL HEMPSTEAD
HERTFORDSHIRE
HP2 7ST

FIRST PUBLISHED BY ARGUS BOOKS 1989
REPRINTED 1990

© PETER HOLLAND 1989
ISBN 0 85242 966 5

PHOTOSETTING BY ISLAND GRAPHICS
PRINTED AND BOUND BY RICHARD CLAY LTD

CONTENTS

Introduction

MODEL making is fun and it doesn't have to be expensive.

The aim of *Amazing Models!* is to show you how you can make working models – of, among others, a dragster, helicopter, rocket, swingwing jet and racing canoe – using only the most simple household materials. You will be amazed when you see what these models can do for little or no cost and with the minimum of assembly time.

In this volume, there are 12 models and a chapter is devoted to each. Each chapter contains a drawing of the finished model, some simple instructions and a series of full-size, detailed drawings which you can copy onto the required materials.

The tools and materials you will need can probably be found around the house and, if not, can be bought cheaply at an art shop, DIY shop or at your local store.

WHAT YOU WILL NEED

A) Tools
– a small sharp modelling knife with a pointed blade
– fine glasspaper (sandpaper) or emery boards
– small "snipe-nosed" pliers
– school compass
– pen and pencil
– ruler
– scissors

B) Materials
– rubber bands
– balsa wood
– woodwork (PVA) or modelling glue
– modelling clay (plasticine)
– 5-minute epoxy adhesive or Superglue

– thin card (corn flake packets, postcards etc)
– thin plastic containers (tubs of margarine etc)
– plastic drinking straws (straight and bendy)
– paper clips
– cocktail sticks (wooden)
– old ballpoint pens
– cotton buds (hollow-stemmed)
– expanded polystyrene ceiling tiles
– greaseproof paper (wax paper)
– pins
– sewing thread

When you have built the models, they can be coloured with felt tip pens or, if they are boats, spray paint from aerosol cans. Masking tape is useful for masking bits off when painting and also for holding parts together during assembly.

MODELLING TIPS

Before you make a start on the first model, you should be aware of some of the simple techniques we will be using throughout this book. In this section, we will show you how to make axles, cranks hooks and hinges from paper clips and ballpoint pens, and also how to transfer shapes from the drawings onto the material, normally balsa wood.

Paper clips

Paper clips can be bent into all sorts of shapes and are strong enough for the very light work involved in these simple and efficient models. All you have to do is to twist and snip with fingers or pliers and you have the basis for the mechanical workings of the models, as shown in the drawing.

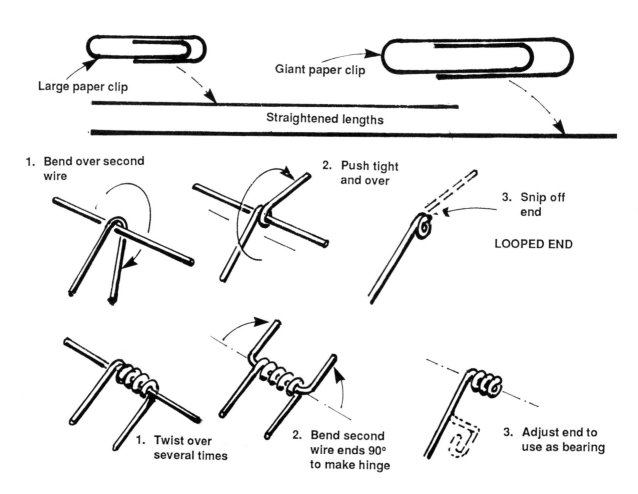

Large paper clip

Giant paper clip

Straightened lengths

1. **Bend over second wire**

2. **Push tight and over**

3. **Snip off end**

LOOPED END

1. **Twist over several times**

2. **Bend second wire ends 90° to make hinge**

3. **Adjust end to use as bearing**

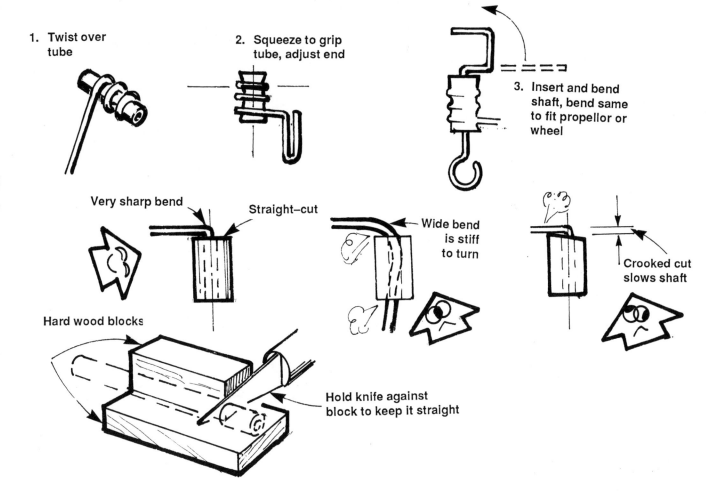

1. Twist over tube

2. Squeeze to grip tube, adjust end

3. Insert and bend shaft, bend same to fit propellor or wheel

Very sharp bend

Straight–cut

Wide bend is stiff to turn

Crooked cut slows shaft

Hard wood blocks

Hold knife against block to keep it straight

Ballpoint pen

The two paper clips make bearings that are fine for axles and cranks but, when a rubber band is hooked up to make a drive like that in a rubber-driven model airplane, the result is unsatisfactory. This is because the wire is pulled hard against the twisty bearing end. This is where the ballpoint pen comes in useful.

The empty nylon tube which once contained ink is perfect for the job. Rip the pen apart by taking the plastic top plug out with a pin and pushing the ink tube up and out. Lay the tube flat on a piece of wood and

cut a slice off the top end and make sure that the cut is straight.

As you can see, the bent end of the wire slides on the level end of the tube, the twisted wire adjusts the tube to fit the shaft and you can now make models driven by twisted rubber bands or band and thread. This is the basis of nearly all the designs in this book.

Cutting balsa wood

Balsa wood shapes are cut with a modelling knife over a flat scrap of wood or hardboard. Thick corrugated

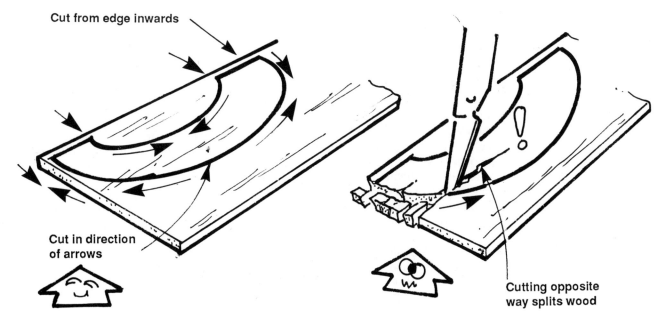

Cut from edge inwards

Cut in direction of arrows

Cutting opposite way splits wood

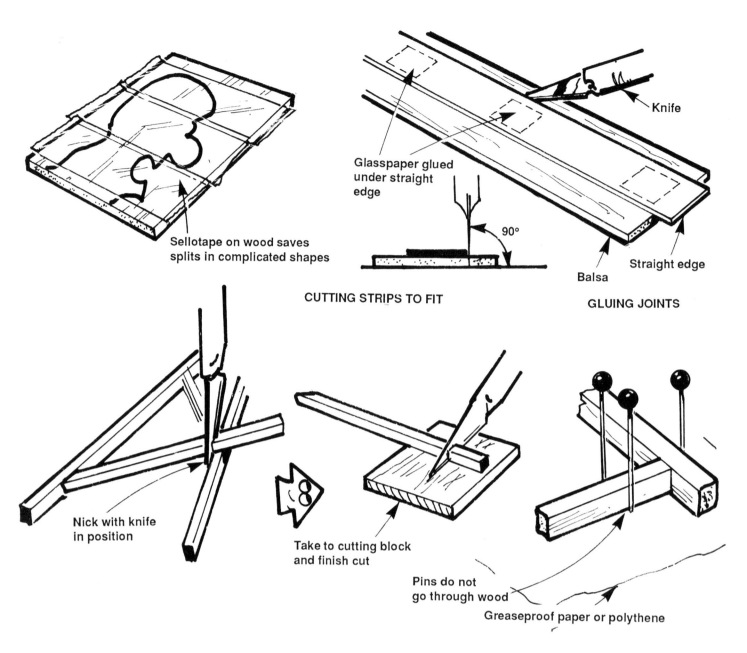

Sellotape on wood saves splits in complicated shapes

Glasspaper glued under straight edge

90°

Knife

Balsa

Straight edge

CUTTING STRIPS TO FIT

GLUING JOINTS

Nick with knife in position

Take to cutting block and finish cut

Pins do not go through wood

Greaseproof paper or polythene

cardboard from grocery boxes will also do. Above are some tips to make balsa cutting easier.

Transferring shapes

1) Carbon. Put a piece of carbon paper over the wood, carbon side down. Place the wood/carbon sandwich under the page you want to copy, positioning it so the edge of the wood is close to a long straight side of the part. Go over the lines with a hard pencil or worn out ballpoint pen and, if the wood has not slipped, the lines will be where they are needed.

2) Tick strips. Take a narrow strip of paper, lay it over the plan and mark the length of each side with a pencil tick. If each dimension is given an identification letter, as shown in the sketches, one strip can serve several measurements. Lay the strip on the wood and transfer the marks. Use a postcard to get the right angles truly 90 degrees.

3) Compasses. You can use these to transfer lengths from plan to wood and you can also use them to transfer angles. Lay the compass flat on its side so that one leg is over one of the lines. Swing the other

leg until it is over the angled line, sliding the compass to get it to match. With one line already on the wood, lay the compass down and use the second leg as a rule to draw the second line with pen or pencil

4) Tracing. Greaseproof paper is transparent enough to see the shapes through and takes pencil or fine felt tip pen lines. Transfer the shapes to the wood by pricking through with a blunt pin, then join up the marks.

Finding the middle

All the circular parts on the plans have the centre marked, so just set the compass. However what happens if a ready-made item, like a plastic lid, is not exactly the right size?

In this case, take a tick strip and mark the diameter by laying the strip across the round item and tick the edges of the circle. Now fold the paper over until the two marks match up. The fold line is half way and is the centre of the circle. This method can also be used to find the centre of a straight line.

Angles can be marked by folding a piece of paper diagonally.

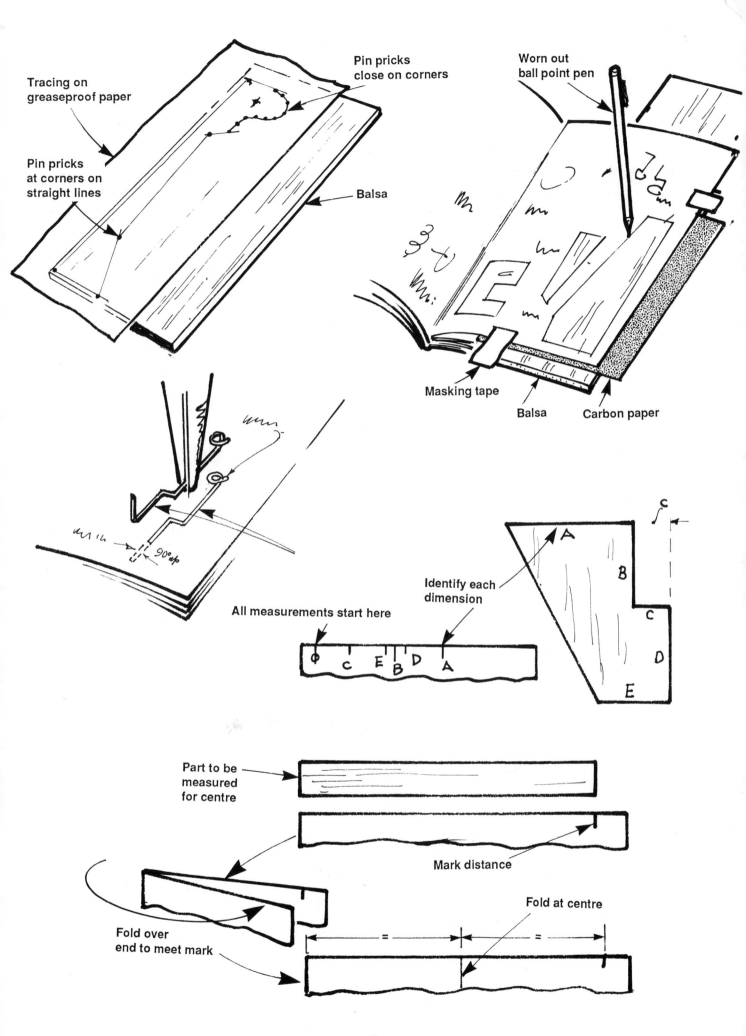

Tracing on greaseproof paper

Pin pricks close on corners

Pin pricks at corners on straight lines

Balsa

Worn out ball point pen

Masking tape

Balsa

Carbon paper

90° up

All measurements start here

Identify each dimension

Part to be measured for centre

Mark distance

Fold over end to meet mark

Fold at centre

7

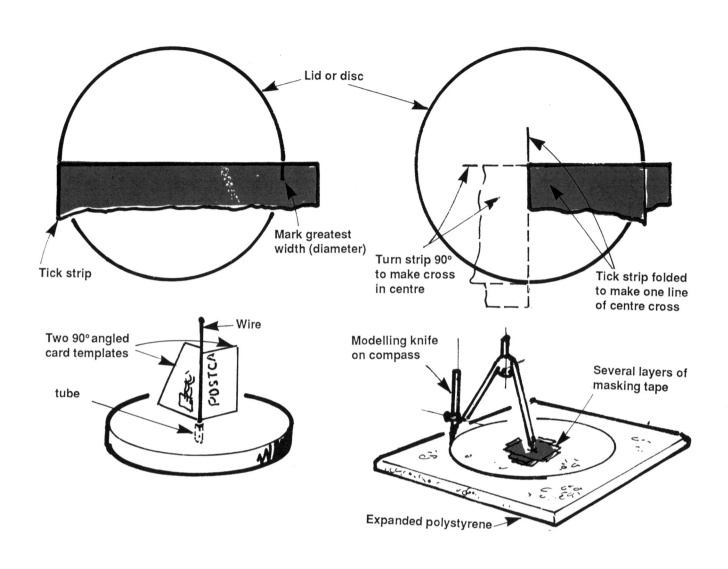

Lid or disc

Tick strip

Mark greatest
width (diameter)

Turn strip 90°
to make cross
in centre

Tick strip folded
to make one line
of centre cross

Two 90° angled
card templates

Wire

tube

POSTCA

Modelling knife
on compass

Several layers of
masking tape

Expanded polystyrene

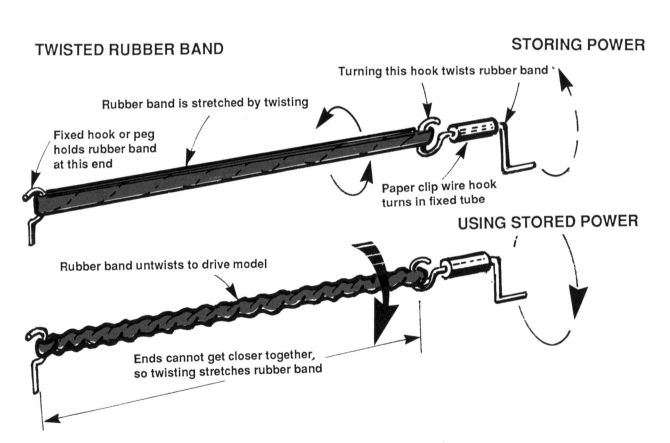

TWISTED RUBBER BAND

STORING POWER

Turning this hook twists rubber band

Rubber band is stretched by twisting

Fixed hook or peg
holds rubber band
at this end

Paper clip wire hook
turns in fixed tube

USING STORED POWER

Rubber band untwists to drive model

Ends cannot get closer together,
so twisting stretches rubber band

Rubber Band Power

How do we get power from something so simple as a rubber band? The first thing that comes to mind is to use the band as a catapult, stretching it to store the energy, then hooking something onto it, so that the energy suddenly gets that "something" moving in a straight line. There are three models that make use of this type of stored energy in this book. They are POGO X2 – a self launching "rocket", JUMP JET which has two catapults for transitional flight and the F1-11 swing wing aircraft which is catapulted, but also uses a rubber band to open the wings.

Making things go round and round
If a rubber band is twisted many times, as demonstrated in the drawings, it can be made to unwind by turning a hook on the end of a crank (bent wire) to make something go round and round or back and forth. Twisting the band stores the energy because, as it is twisted, it is stretched.

The first model ORBITER demonstrates this method. There are several others, like HELITWISTERS, which are simple flying machines, or 3-POINTER, an interesting boat with three floats.

The rubber band can also be stretched lengthwise and attached to a piece of cotton. One end of the band is fixed and the other end of the cotton can be wound up on a wire shaft or straightened paper clip. As the cotton is wound on the wire, the band gets stretched, so energy is stored.

The rubber band then pulls at the cotton, unwinding it from the wire, so the wire turns to drive the model. The second pair of drawings explains this. WHEELER is a model that demonstrates the system and most of the other models in this book use it.

STRETCHED RUBBER BAND

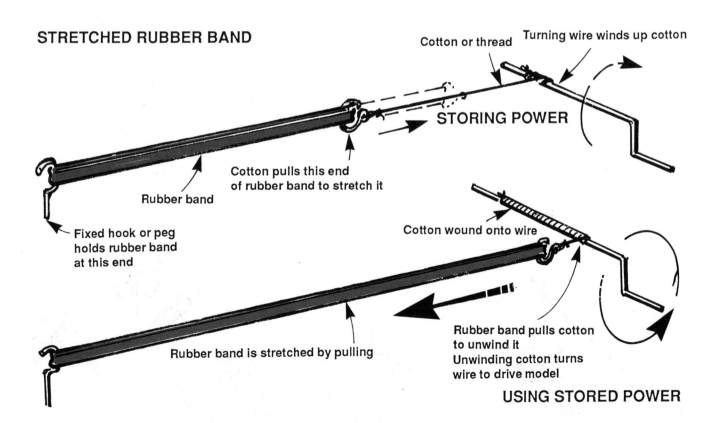

Cotton or thread

Turning wire winds up cotton

STORING POWER

Cotton pulls this end of rubber band to stretch it

Rubber band

Fixed hook or peg holds rubber band at this end

Cotton wound onto wire

Rubber band is stretched by pulling

Rubber band pulls cotton to unwind it
Unwinding cotton turns wire to drive model

USING STORED POWER

1 Orbiter

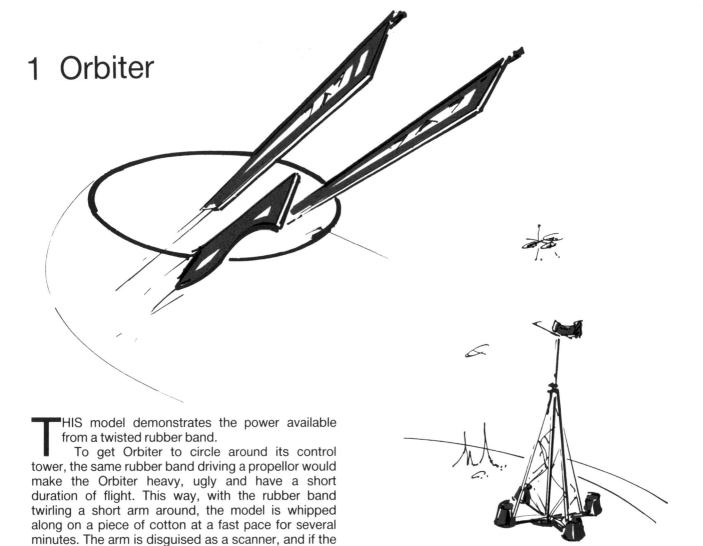

THIS model demonstrates the power available from a twisted rubber band.

To get Orbiter to circle around its control tower, the same rubber band driving a propellor would make the Orbiter heavy, ugly and have a short duration of flight. This way, with the rubber band twirling a short arm around, the model is whipped along on a piece of cotton at a fast pace for several minutes. The arm is disguised as a scanner, and if the cotton is that nearly invisible nylon mending monofiliment, the illusion is complete.

ASSEMBLY

Get some balsa wood strip 4×3mm (³⁄₁₆″×⅛″) and 4×1.5mm (³⁄₁₆″×¹⁄₁₆″) or cut your own strip from sheet balsa using a metal straight-edge. You will also need a small amount of balsa sheet 1.5mm (¹⁄₁₆″) thick. Use thick paper to roll short tubes and for the scanner Panel, as shown in the drawing.

The thin, light, springy plastic cut from the bottom of a cheese spread segments container, is just right for the disc of the Orbiter craft itself.

The tower

Make the paper tubes first (below) as they can be drying while the woodwork is done. Cut the strips of balsa to length by laying them in place and trimming off to length.

Four frames are needed to make the tower, joined as shown and fitted with the balsa and tube top cap.

Make the wire arm/hook from a giant size paper clip which also acts as a winding arm. Disconnect the cotton from the arm while winding.

The craft

Using a compass, mark out a circle on the cheese box plastic. This must be flat or the slight bend added later will not be right.

Cut the probes and gondola from 1.5mm (¹⁄₁₆″) balsa and glue them to the disc. Pierce for the cotton and spend some time adjusting the balance by positioning the panel pins and modelling clay on the probes. This, and the slight tilt to the rear edge of the disc, can be adjusted until the craft can be hand-glided onto a soft surface. It should go straight and long. Avoid short nose-dives or short swoops and switchbacks. This craft really glides. When hooked up to the wound-up arm via cotton and launched level at the same height, it should accelerate smoothly and continue flying until the rubber runs down.

TUBE ROLLING

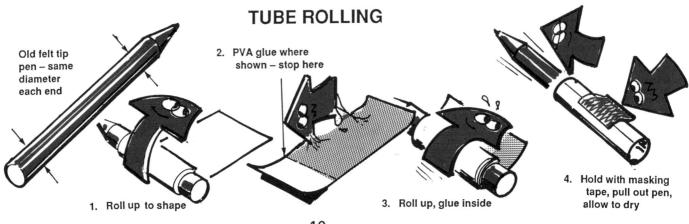

Old felt tip pen – same diameter each end

1. **Roll up to shape**

2. PVA glue where shown – stop here

3. **Roll up, glue inside**

4. **Hold with masking tape, pull out pen, allow to dry**

10

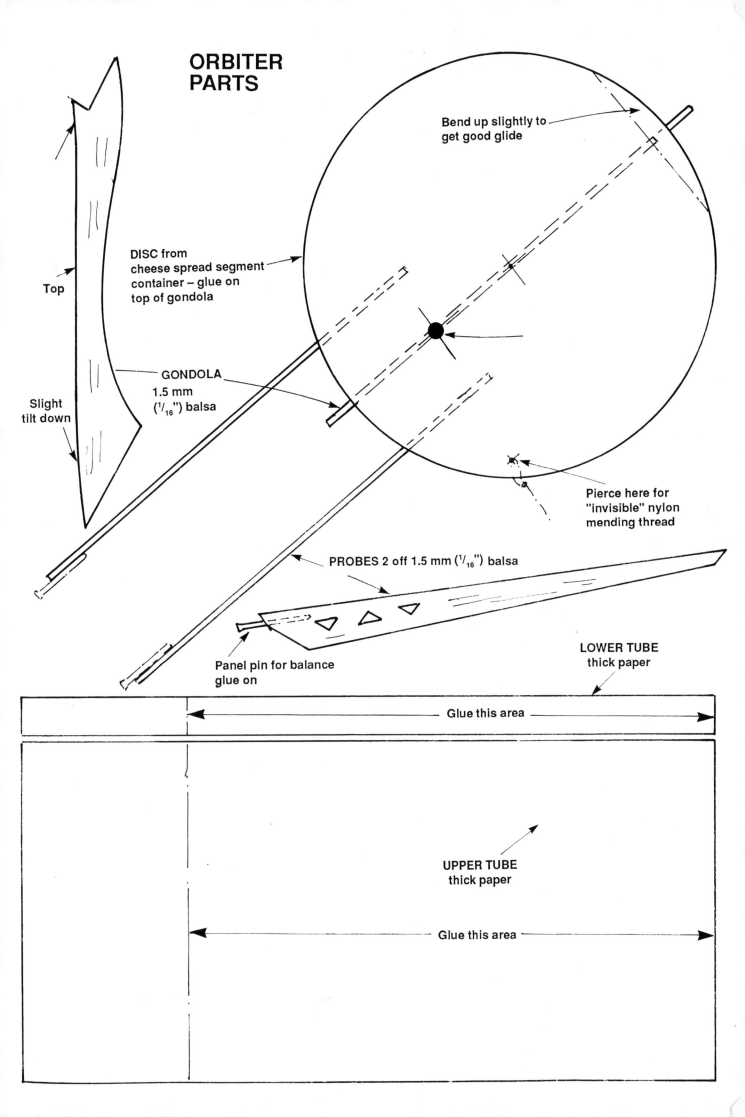

ORBITER PARTS

Top

Slight tilt down

DISC from cheese spread segment container – glue on top of gondola

GONDOLA 1.5 mm ($^1/_{16}$") balsa

Bend up slightly to get good glide

Pierce here for "invisible" nylon mending thread

PROBES 2 off 1.5 mm ($^1/_{16}$") balsa

Panel pin for balance glue on

LOWER TUBE thick paper

Glue this area

UPPER TUBE thick paper

Glue this area

ORBITER PARTS AND ASSEMBLY

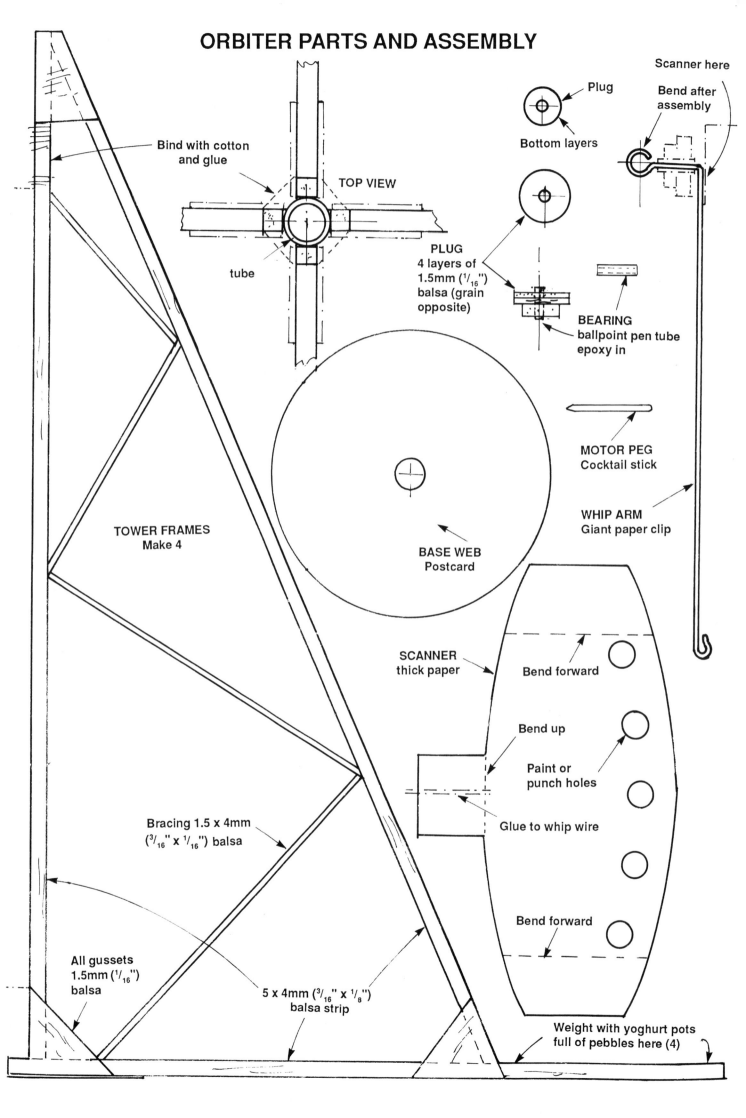

Bind with cotton and glue

TOP VIEW

tube

Plug

Bottom layers

Scanner here

Bend after assembly

PLUG
4 layers of 1.5mm (1/16") balsa (grain opposite)

BEARING
ballpoint pen tube epoxy in

MOTOR PEG
Cocktail stick

WHIP ARM
Giant paper clip

TOWER FRAMES
Make 4

BASE WEB
Postcard

SCANNER
thick paper

Bend forward

Bend up

Paint or punch holes

Glue to whip wire

Bracing 1.5 x 4mm (3/16" x 1/16") balsa

Bend forward

All gussets 1.5mm (1/16") balsa

5 x 4mm (3/16" x 1/8") balsa strip

Weight with yoghurt pots full of pebbles here (4)

ORBITER ASSEMBLY

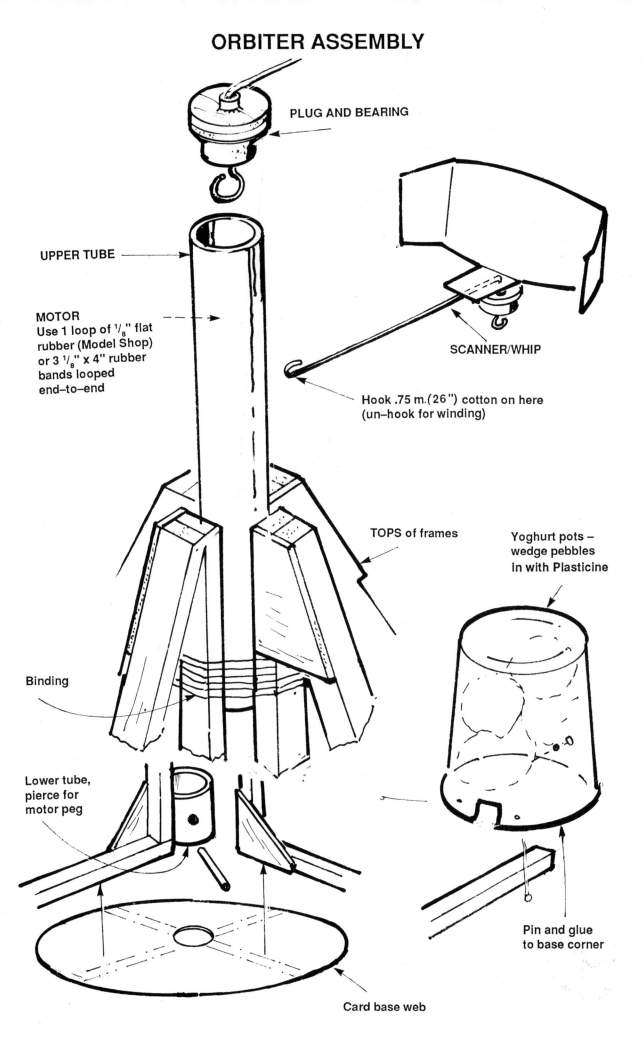

PLUG AND BEARING

UPPER TUBE

MOTOR
Use 1 loop of 1/8" flat
rubber (Model Shop)
or 3 1/8" x 4" rubber
bands looped
end–to–end

SCANNER/WHIP

Hook .75 m. (26") cotton on here
(un–hook for winding)

TOPS of frames

Yoghurt pots –
wedge pebbles
in with Plasticine

Binding

Lower tube,
pierce for
motor peg

Pin and glue
to base corner

Card base web

13

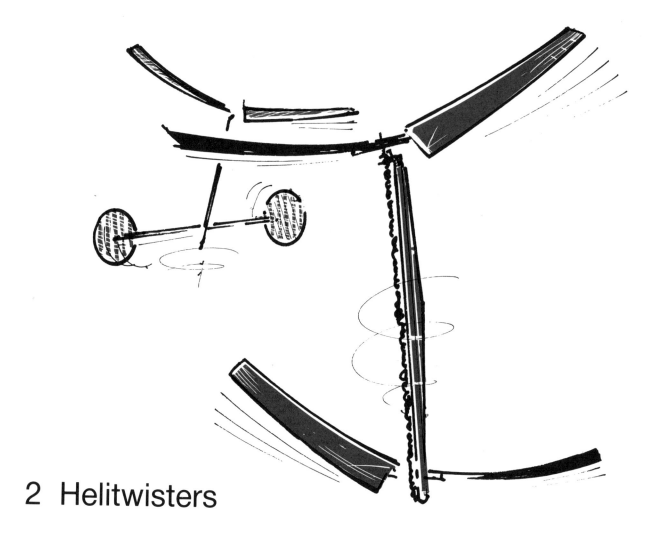

2 Helitwisters

THESE two simple machines are helicopters designed for flying indoors or, in calm weather, outside. A rubber band does the work and the rotors turn in opposite directions.

ASSEMBLY

The materials are balsa wood – small pieces of 5mm (¼″) square and 4mm (³⁄₁₆″) square strip, 0.8mm (¹⁄₃₂″) and 1.5mm (¹⁄₁₆″) sheet and 3mm (¹⁄₈″) square strip.

Cut the blades from 0.8mm sheet and add the root doublers on the top surface. Two blades go at the top for counter-clockwise rotation, and two at the bottom are a mirror image for the opposite rotating lower rotor on Model 1, shown large in the heading sketch. The smaller Helitwister (2), does not need the lower ones;

there is a bar with paper paddles instead.

Take care to make the hub strips (5mm (¼″) square strip) just right. The corners shaved off from opposite corners of the lower face make the blades sit at the correct tilt and twist. Get it wrong and they will suck instead of blow, or just do nothing!

The lower rotor, or the "Paddle bar" on Helitwister 2, is held in place with a tiny rubber band, so that it is shock-absorbing and less likely to break when the model lands.

Do not use more than the indicated size rubber bands. The stick will break. Stronger sticks are heavier, so the machine hits harder when it lands.

Experiment by twisting the blade tips flatter for more revs, or by creasing the paper paddles to control Helitwister 2.

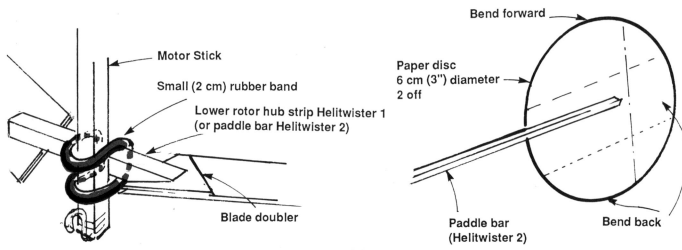

14

HELITWISTERS PARTS AND ASSEMBLY

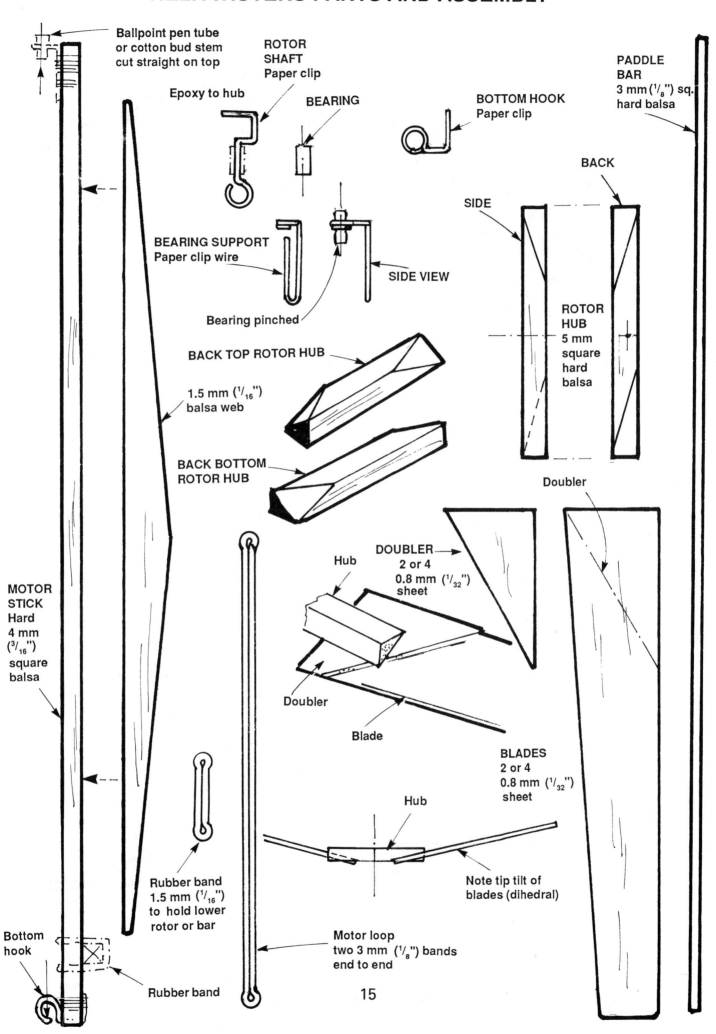

Ballpoint pen tube or cotton bud stem cut straight on top

ROTOR SHAFT
Paper clip
Epoxy to hub

BEARING

BOTTOM HOOK
Paper clip

PADDLE BAR
3 mm ($^1/_8$") sq. hard balsa

BEARING SUPPORT
Paper clip wire

SIDE VIEW

Bearing pinched

BACK

SIDE

BACK TOP ROTOR HUB

ROTOR HUB
5 mm square hard balsa

1.5 mm ($^1/_{16}$") balsa web

BACK BOTTOM ROTOR HUB

Doubler

DOUBLER
2 or 4
0.8 mm ($^1/_{32}$") sheet

MOTOR STICK
Hard
4 mm ($^3/_{16}$") square balsa

Hub

Doubler

Blade

BLADES
2 or 4
0.8 mm ($^1/_{32}$") sheet

Hub

Rubber band
1.5 mm ($^1/_{16}$") to hold lower rotor or bar

Note tip tilt of blades (dihedral)

Bottom hook

Rubber band

Motor loop
two 3 mm ($^1/_8$") bands end to end

15

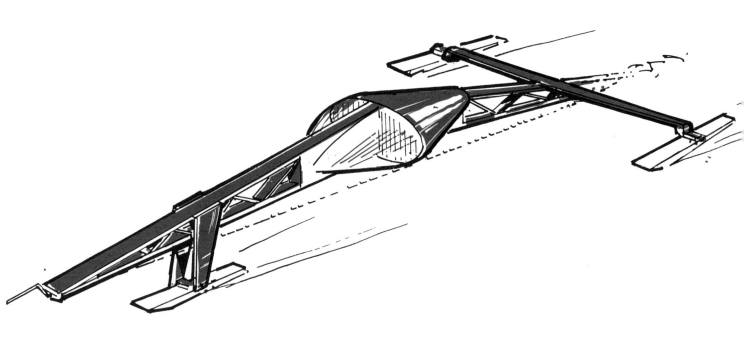

3 Three-pointer

NOW take to the water. Make this space-age, space frame machine which adjusts its floats to match the ripples of the water. It is driven along by a self-adjusting propellor, powered by more rubber bands.

ASSEMBLY

Little balsa wood is needed, because there is no hull. After copying the frame shapes onto greaseproof paper, you can start building. Use thick paper for the cabin, with scrap clear plastic (bubble pack waste), for the windscreens. The floats are scraps of expanded polystyrene ceiling tile and the propellor is thick margarine tub plastic.

Make the two beam parts, taking care to cut the diagonal spacers from the thinner strip, as this craft must be light. Join up the beam halves so that there is a distinct "hump" to clear the water. Postcard is strong enough to reinforce the centre joint but

waterproof it after assembly with modelling paint or varnish. Do not paint the floats as most model paints melt them. The propellor shaft has a small kink in it to run on the end of the bearing tube. Bend the shaft until the doubled back end spins true. Now the propellor blade shape can be epoxied in place. The curved front edges lean forward when the plastic is folded. This causes the blades to go into a "coarse" pitch when there is plenty of power in the rubber motor, then to flatten to a "fine" pitch to keep the revs-per-minute about the same when there is less power.

Wind the finished model by first inserting a cocktail stick or matchstick into the prop shaft loop next to the rubber. This forms a brake. Wind on the turns from the handle at the front and lock this end with a match stick in the same way.

Place the craft on the water and pull out the rear "brake" matchstick.

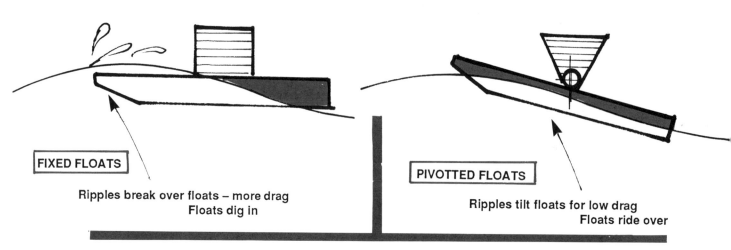

FIXED FLOATS

Ripples break over floats – more drag
Floats dig in

PIVOTTED FLOATS

Ripples tilt floats for low drag
Floats ride over

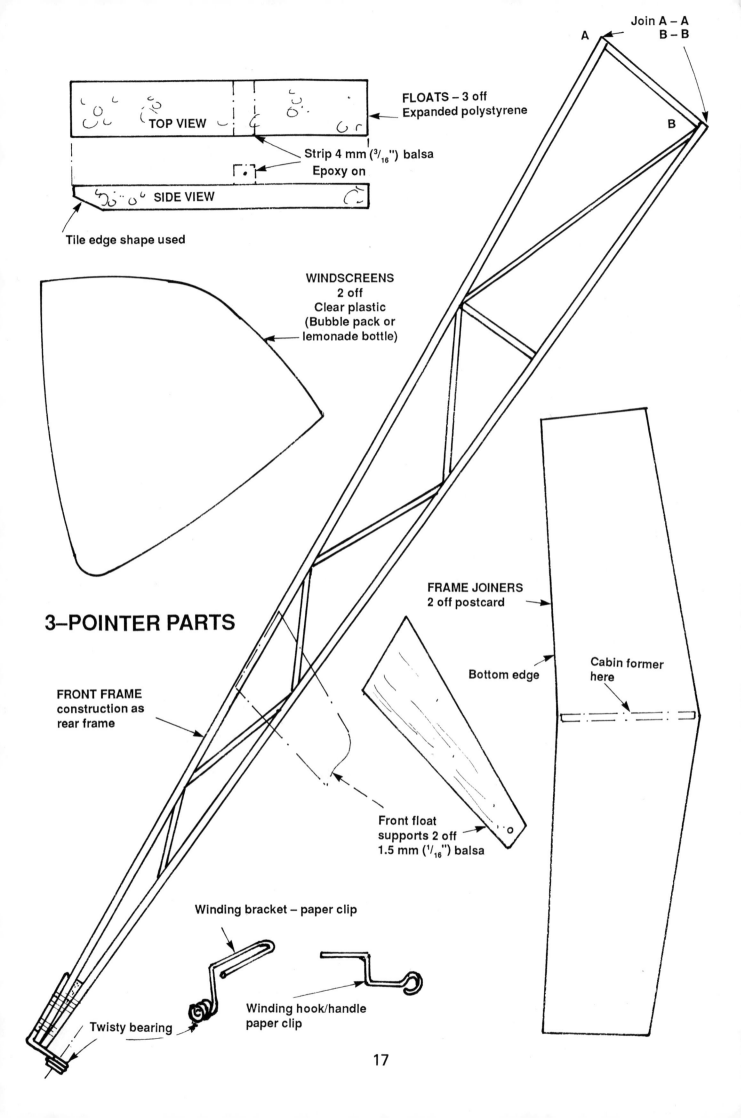

FLOATS – 3 off
Expanded polystyrene

TOP VIEW

Strip 4 mm ($^3/_{16}$") balsa
Epoxy on

SIDE VIEW

Tile edge shape used

WINDSCREENS
2 off
Clear plastic
(Bubble pack or
lemonade bottle)

Join A – A
B – B

A

B

FRAME JOINERS
2 off postcard

Bottom edge

Cabin former
here

3–POINTER PARTS

FRONT FRAME
construction as
rear frame

Front float
supports 2 off
1.5 mm ($^1/_{16}$") balsa

Winding bracket – paper clip

Twisty bearing

Winding hook/handle
paper clip

3–POINTER PARTS

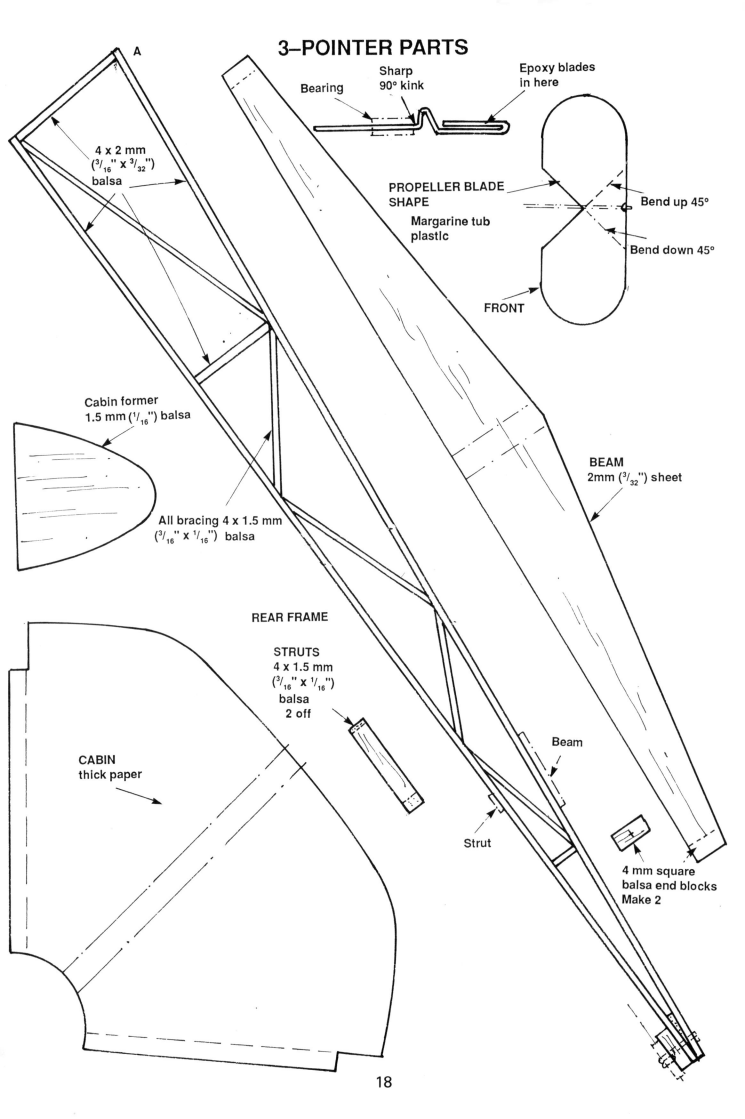

A

4 x 2 mm
($\frac{3}{16}$" x $\frac{3}{32}$")
balsa

Bearing

Sharp 90° kink

Epoxy blades in here

PROPELLER BLADE SHAPE

Margarine tub plastic

Bend up 45°

Bend down 45°

FRONT

Cabin former
1.5 mm ($\frac{1}{16}$") balsa

BEAM
2mm ($\frac{3}{32}$") sheet

All bracing 4 x 1.5 mm
($\frac{3}{16}$" x $\frac{1}{16}$") balsa

REAR FRAME

STRUTS
4 x 1.5 mm
($\frac{3}{16}$" x $\frac{1}{16}$")
balsa
2 off

Beam

CABIN
thick paper

Strut

4 mm square
balsa end blocks
Make 2

3 – POINTER ASSEMBLY

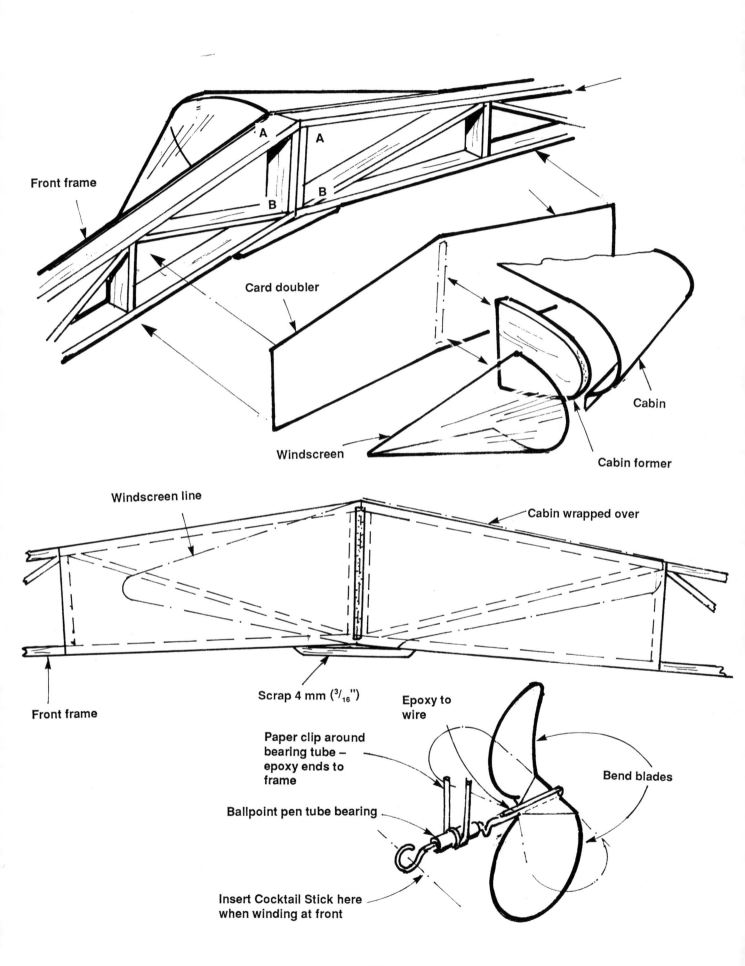

Front frame

A A

B B

Card doubler

Cabin

Windscreen

Cabin former

Windscreen line

Cabin wrapped over

Front frame

Scrap 4 mm ($^3/_{16}$")

Epoxy to wire

Paper clip around bearing tube – epoxy ends to frame

Bend blades

Ballpoint pen tube bearing

Insert Cocktail Stick here when winding at front

3 – POINTER ASSEMBLY

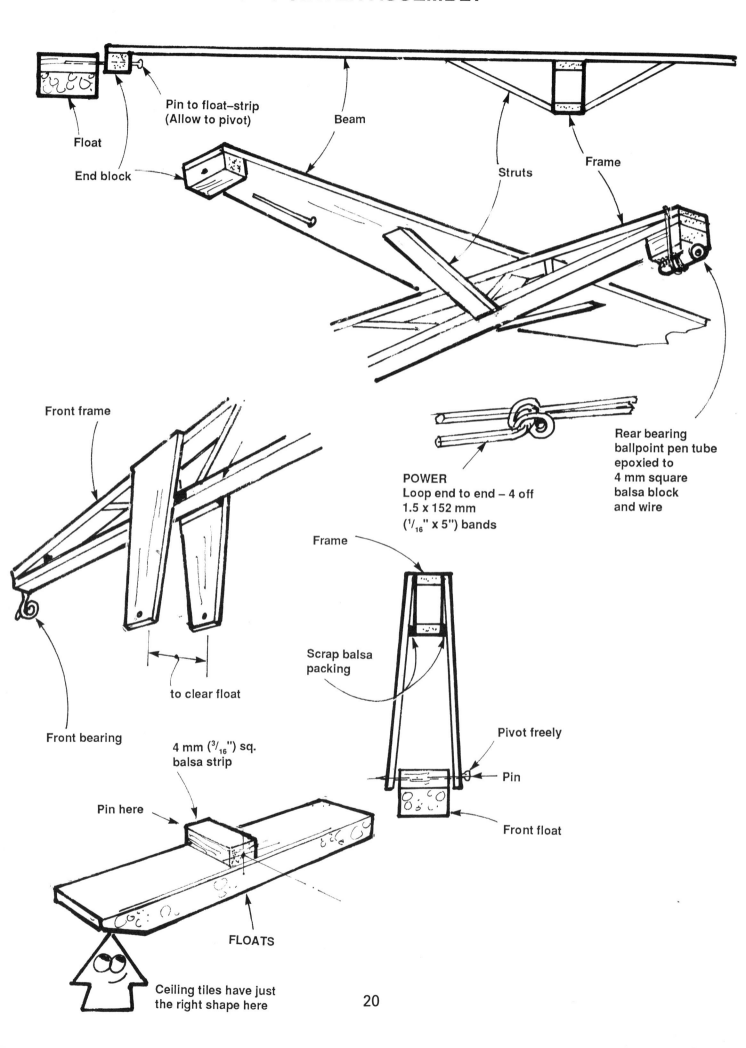

Pin to float–strip
(Allow to pivot)

Beam

Float

End block

Struts

Frame

Front frame

POWER
Loop end to end – 4 off
1.5 x 152 mm
($^1/_{16}$" x 5") bands

Rear bearing
ballpoint pen tube
epoxied to
4 mm square
balsa block
and wire

Frame

Scrap balsa
packing

to clear float

Pivot freely

Pin

Front bearing

4 mm ($^3/_{16}$") sq.
balsa strip

Pin here

Front float

FLOATS

Ceiling tiles have just
the right shape here

20

4 Wheeler

THE power stored in a stretched rubber band can be used in other ways than by twisting it. A band can pull a piece of cotton or thread wound up on an axle or shaft and, in doing this, it is stretched about three times its length. However, this can be quite difficult to get into some models, particularly something as compact as the Wheeler.

In order to have the axle where it should be, the end of the band would have to be way outside the machine. Luckily the power is small, so the cotton can be doubled back through a smooth paper clip loop end, then the whole length can be used.

Even better, the same power can be provided for twice the length of run by the use of a couple of bands, or one of twice the thickness. Then, with another paper clip loop, this time on the rubber band, it has twice the length of cotton to pull, all in the same length of model. If the cotton is thin, more turns can be carried on a given length of axle so use the thinnest, strongest cotton or thread for the job.

A wide axle will bend, but making it thicker to stand the strain only takes up more cotton, so it does not take enough turns before the band is fully stretched (more cotton used per turn).

Sometimes, the system stalls before the band is fully "run down". It needs greater leverage to do the work, like having a larger diameter axle. The cotton itself can do this. Wind on some extra layers at one end to thicken it, then start to wind the correct length of cotton over the top of this winding. Continue to wind the cotton onto the bare shaft for the more powerful stretch. This is the same principle as changing gear in a car.

Wheeler is one of those strange vehicles which depends on moving a weight in order to drive itself along. In this case, the weight is a small nail in the front of a strip of wood carrying the rubber power unit.

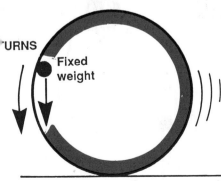

THIS WHEEL ONLY TURNS PART WAY ROUND

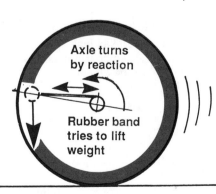

THIS ONE KEEPS GOING WHILE THE RUBBER BAND IS STRETCHED

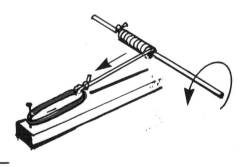

RUBBER BAND UNWINDS COTTON TO TURN SHAFT

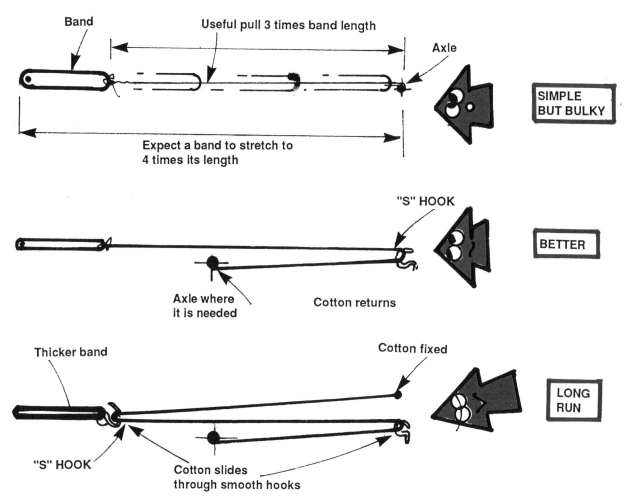

Band

Useful pull 3 times band length

Axle

Expect a band to stretch to
4 times its length

SIMPLE BUT BULKY

"S" HOOK

Axle where it is needed

Cotton returns

BETTER

Thicker band

Cotton fixed

"S" HOOK

Cotton slides through smooth hooks

LONG RUN

ASSEMBLY

The beam

Make from hard grade balsa wood strip and scraps of sheet to the sections and sizes shown on the Parts pages. Cotton bud or ballpoint pen inner tube pieces form long bearings which also space the wheels apart for stability. The cotton may run up tight against the bearings and stop the action. This can be prevented by putting a couple of pins into the wood to reverse the cotton turns to pile over the first, if it gets too close.

The wheels

Cut out expanded polystyrene tiles by clamping a modelling knife in place of the pencil in the compasses. First reinforce the area where the compass point is to go, by gluing one hub disc in place with 5-minute epoxy, or stick several layers of masking tape in the centre.

With both hub discs in position, push a wire through and set up with postcards or set-squares to keep it true while the glue sets. The wire is temporary, so grease or wax it (chinagraph pencil) to make it pull out. Then, true-up the rim which will probably be rather bumpy and off centre.

A wheel lathe

This will be useful for all the expanded polystyrene wheels in this book. On this model, the intention is to get a long run on a small rubber band. If the rims of the wheels are rough or lumpy, it will not go far. Run it on a smooth surface – a polished floor is fine. Treat the Wheeler with care. The axle is thin and the wheels will go wobbly if it is hurriedly wound up. Hold it by the end of the central stick and turn the handle slowly.

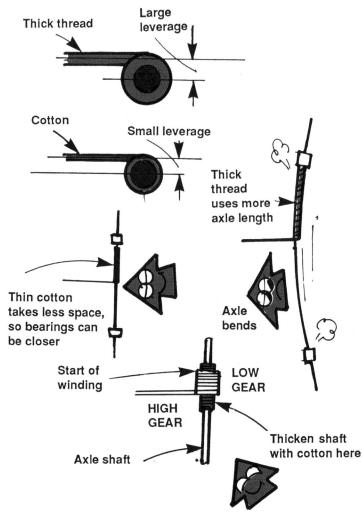

Thick thread

Large leverage

Cotton

Small leverage

Thick thread uses more axle length

Thin cotton takes less space, so bearings can be closer

Axle bends

Start of winding

LOW GEAR

HIGH GEAR

Axle shaft

Thicken shaft with cotton here

WHEELER ASSEMBLY

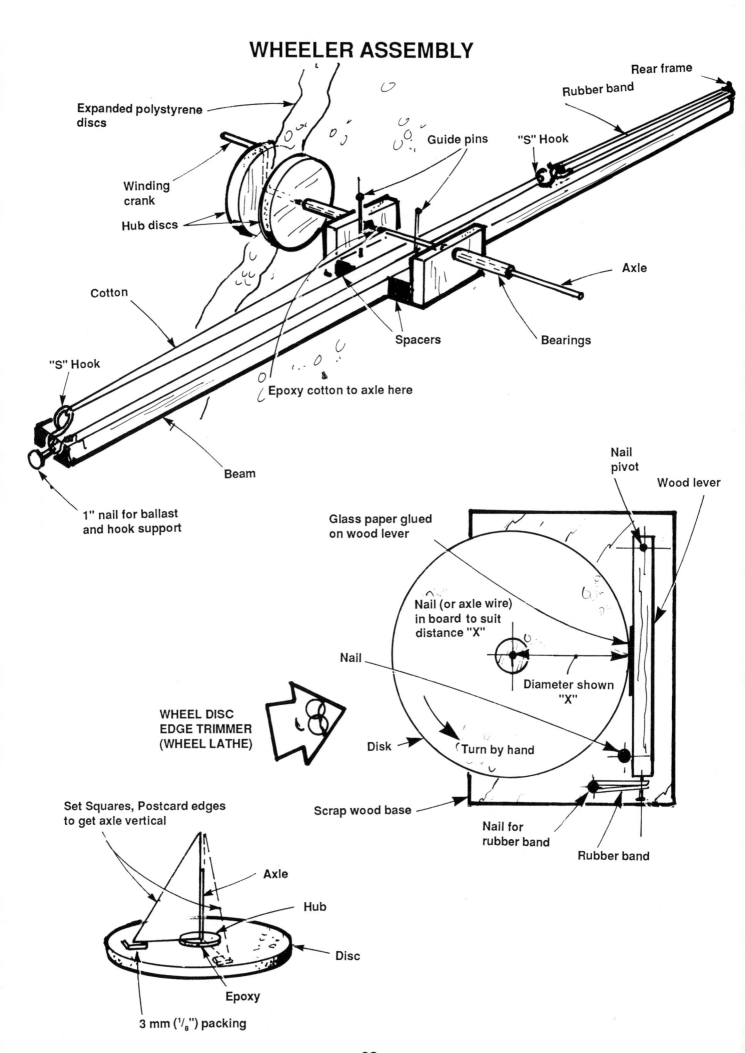

Expanded polystyrene discs

Rear frame

Rubber band

Guide pins

"S" Hook

Winding crank

Hub discs

Axle

Cotton

Spacers

Bearings

"S" Hook

Epoxy cotton to axle here

Beam

1" nail for ballast and hook support

Nail pivot

Wood lever

Glass paper glued on wood lever

Nail (or axle wire) in board to suit distance "X"

Nail

Diameter shown "X"

WHEEL DISC EDGE TRIMMER (WHEEL LATHE)

Disk

Turn by hand

Scrap wood base

Nail for rubber band

Rubber band

Set Squares, Postcard edges to get axle vertical

Axle

Hub

Disc

Epoxy

3 mm ($^1/_8$") packing

WHEELER PARTS

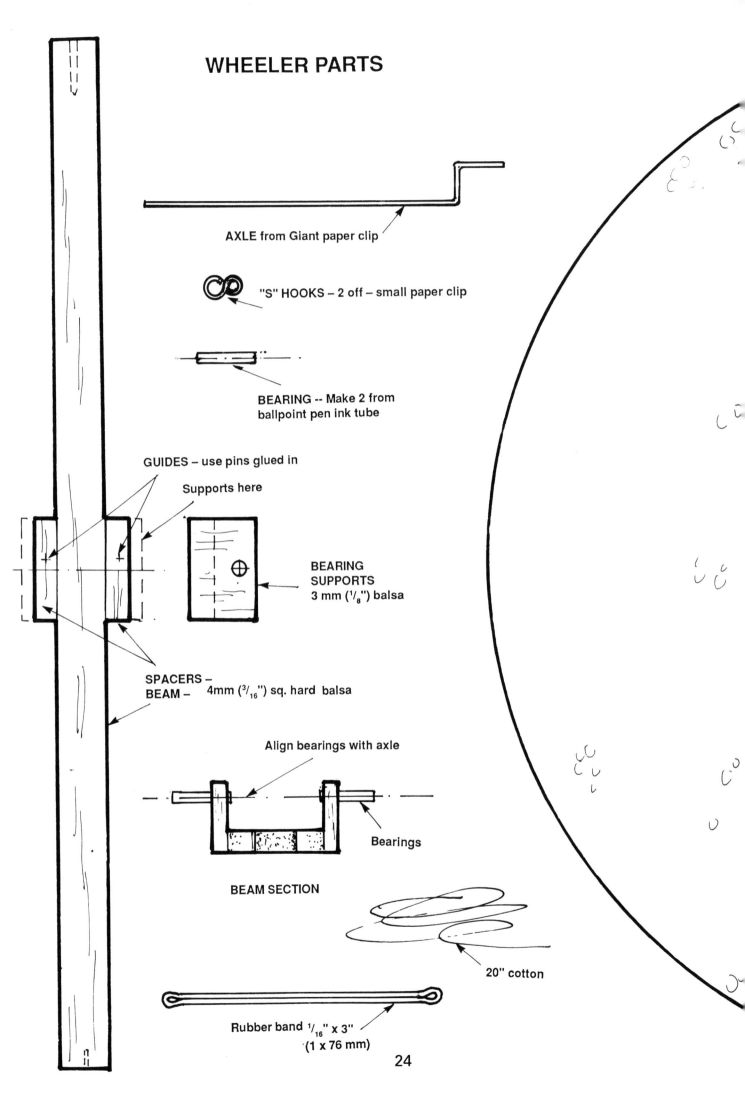

AXLE from Giant paper clip

"S" HOOKS – 2 off – small paper clip

BEARING -- Make 2 from
ballpoint pen ink tube

GUIDES – use pins glued in

Supports here

BEARING
SUPPORTS
3 mm ($\frac{1}{8}$") balsa

SPACERS –
BEAM – 4mm ($\frac{3}{16}$") sq. hard balsa

Align bearings with axle

Bearings

BEAM SECTION

20" cotton

Rubber band $\frac{1}{16}$" x 3"
(1 x 76 mm)

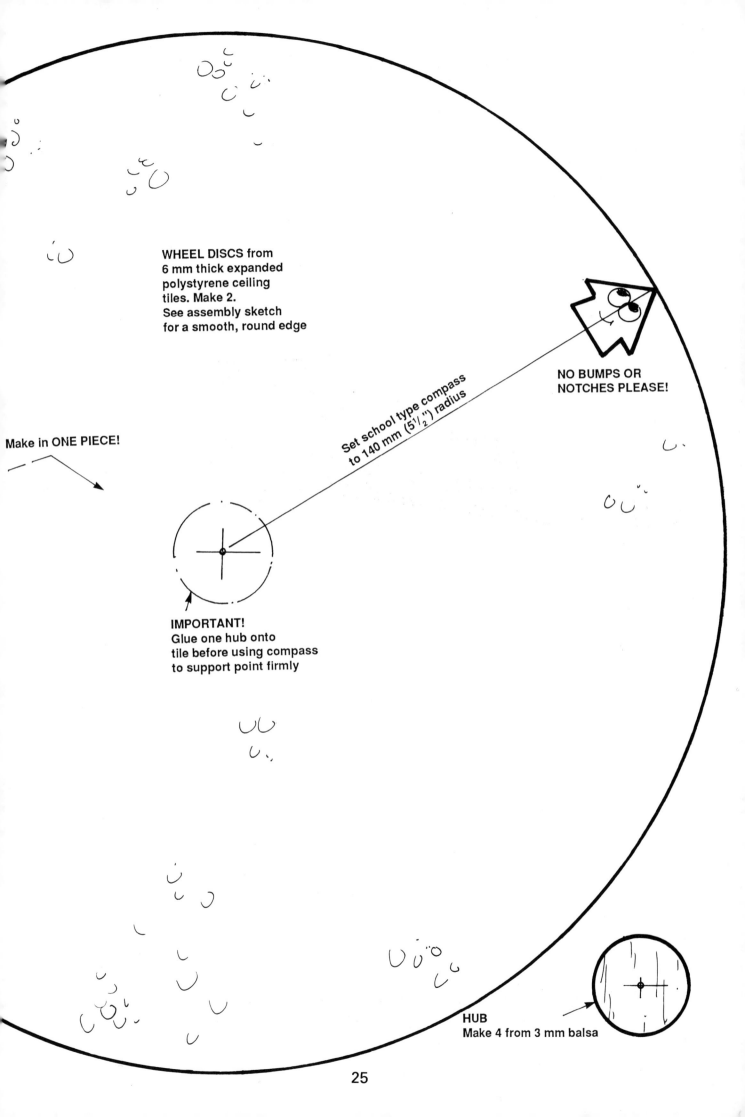

WHEEL DISCS from
6 mm thick expanded
polystyrene ceiling
tiles. Make 2.
See assembly sketch
for a smooth, round edge

NO BUMPS OR
NOTCHES PLEASE!

Set school type compass
to 140 mm (5½") radius

Make in ONE PIECE!

IMPORTANT!
Glue one hub onto
tile before using compass
to support point firmly

HUB
Make 4 from 3 mm balsa

5 Fantastelastic Dragster

THE drive wheels for the Dragster are small empty baked bean cans with the lids replaced. The rest is made from balsa wood, paper clips and other oddments. The chassis is long, so that a simple straight band pull can be used. Dragsters were never intended for marathons.

The Dragster has three modes. In mode 1, the model can be made to coast on after the rubber band has run down, because the thread (not cotton) can slip off the axle, leaving the spinning bean cans to act like flywheels to keep it going for longer.

In mode 2, the thread is hooked firmly and Fantastelastic reverses back some of the way. The impetus of the wheels rewinds the thread the other way. Then, as it unwinds for a second time, it reverses.

In mode 3, the thread slips off but a parachute brake is deployed as a special effect. The sequence sketches on page 30 explain all.

ASSEMBLY

The simple balsa wood bodywork/chassis is reinforced near the axle bearings. There is no need to drill holes in the side pieces, "V" notches in the joint edges being less likely to split the wood. Once the sides are joined on the reinforcing pieces, they are stronger and the holes can be pierced right through.

Although a giant or larger paper clip is strong enough to withstand the pull of the thread and band, 14-gauge (s.w.g) piano wire (from the model shop) is tougher and will withstand knocks better. However, it will be less easy to cut to length. This is not a job for small pliers, so perhaps the household tool kit has a strong pair with cutting edges, or perhaps there is a file. Otherwise the hacksaw may get a little blunt.

Roughen the wire and area around the punched holes in the cans and lids before fixing together with 5-minute epoxy. When they are lined up properly and spinning true, leave them to harden for several hours.

FANTASTELASTIC PARTS

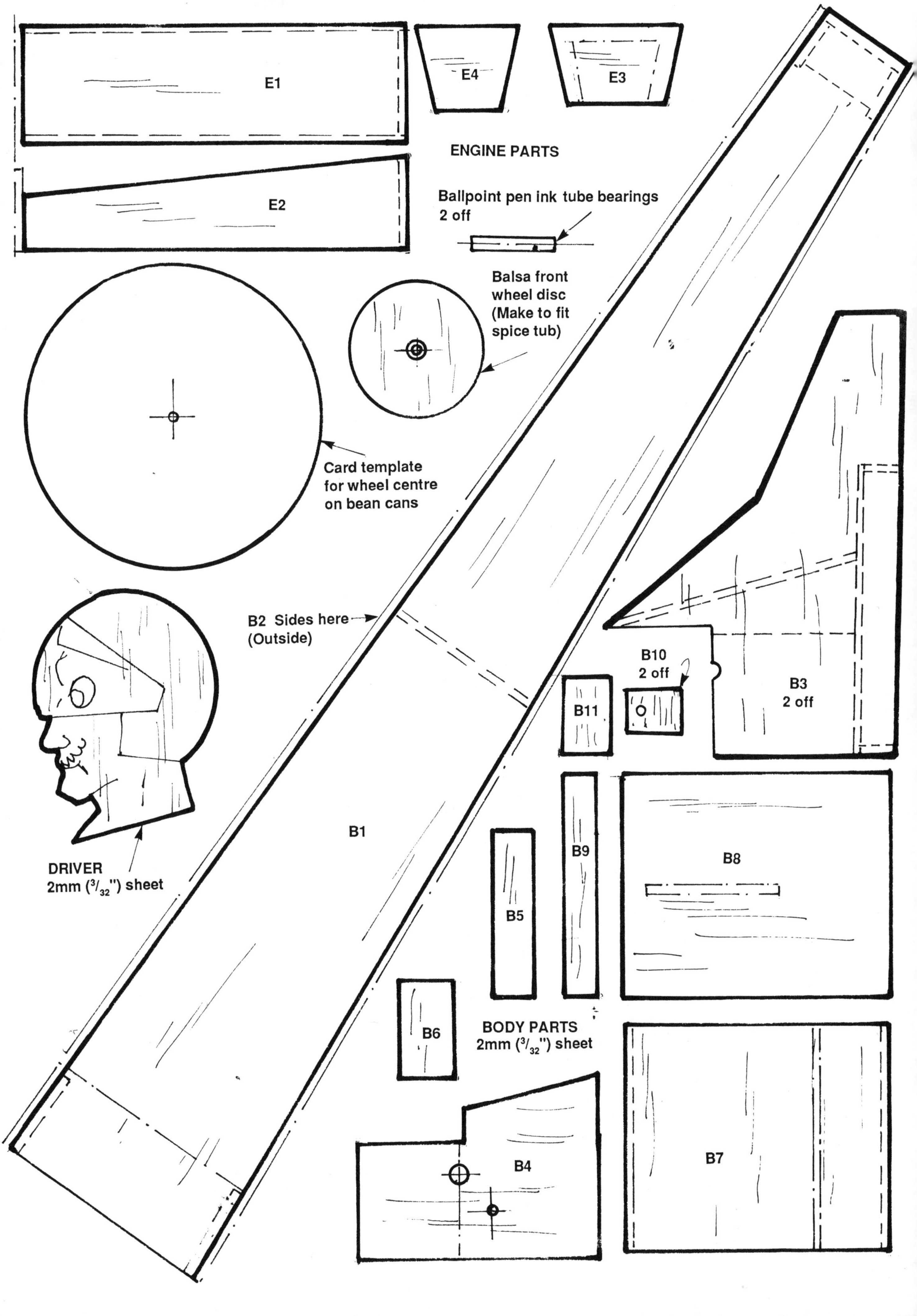

E1

E2

E4

E3

ENGINE PARTS

Ballpoint pen ink tube bearings
2 off

Balsa front
wheel disc
(Make to fit
spice tub)

Card template
for wheel centre
on bean cans

B2 Sides here
(Outside)

B1

DRIVER
2mm ($^3/_{32}$") sheet

B10
2 off

B11

B3
2 off

B9

B5

B8

B6

BODY PARTS
2mm ($^3/_{32}$") sheet

B4

B7

FANTASTELASTIC PARTS/ASSEMBLY

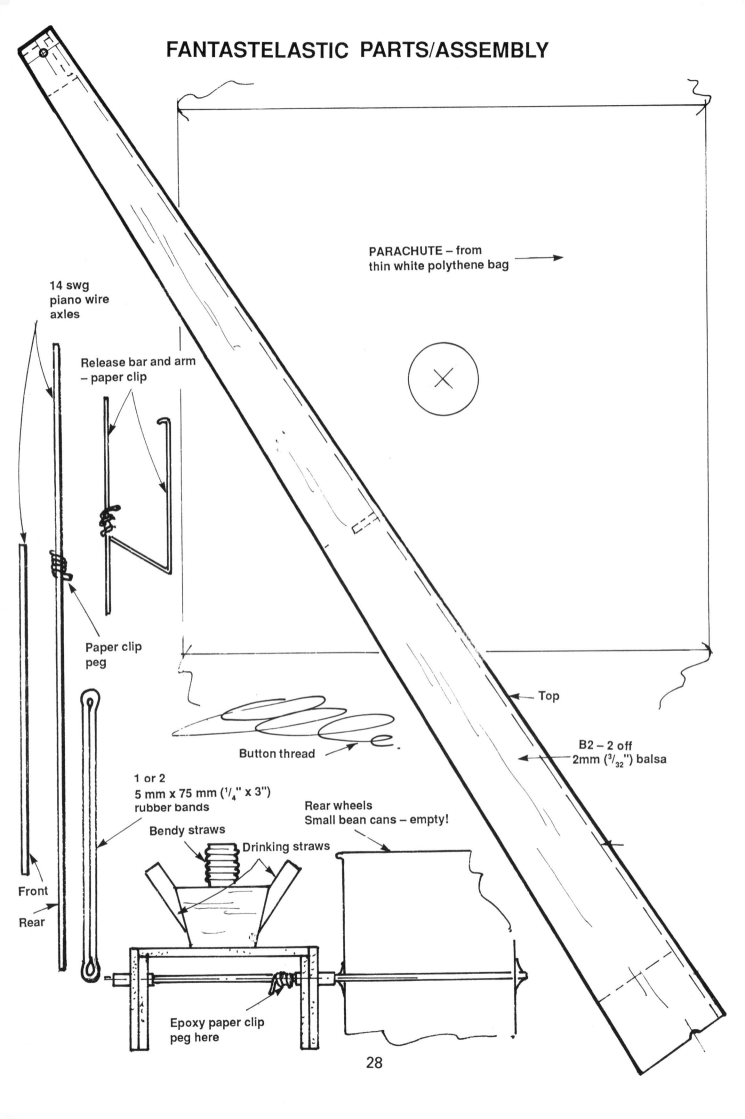

PARACHUTE – from thin white polythene bag

14 swg piano wire axles

Release bar and arm – paper clip

Paper clip peg

Top

B2 – 2 off 2mm ($^3/_{32}$") balsa

Button thread

1 or 2 5 mm x 75 mm ($^1/_4$" x 3") rubber bands

Bendy straws

Drinking straws

Rear wheels Small bean cans – empty!

Front

Rear

Epoxy paper clip peg here

FANTASTELASTIC ASSEMBLY

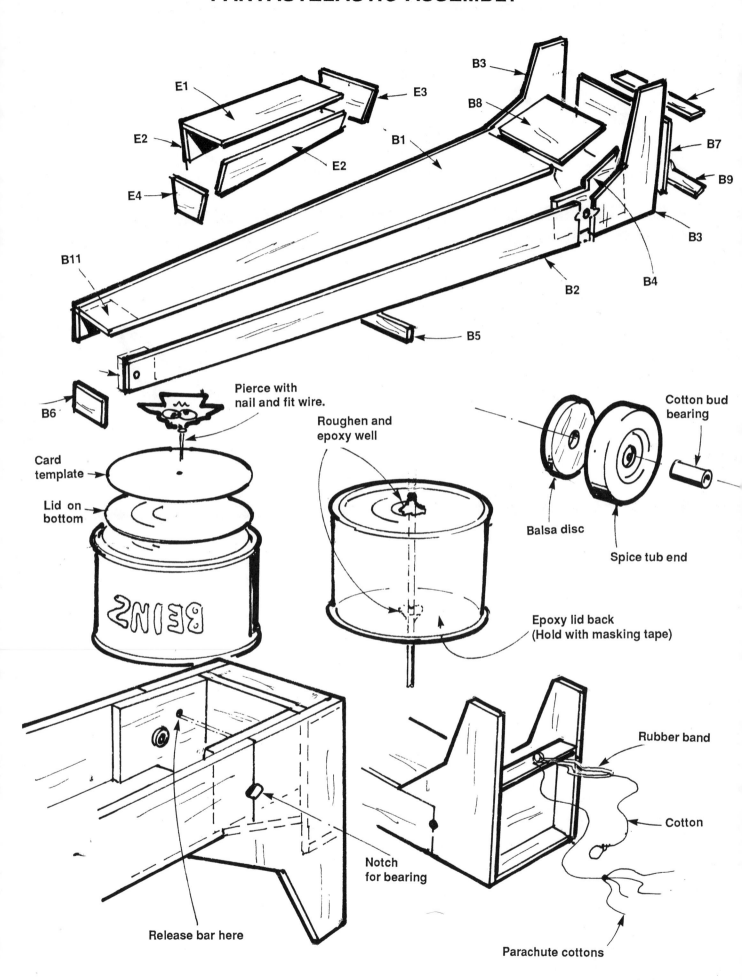

E1

E3

E2

E2

E4

B3

B8

B1

B7

B9

B3

B4

B2

B11

B5

B6

Pierce with
nail and fit wire.

Roughen and
epoxy well

Cotton bud
bearing

Card
template

Lid on
bottom

BEINZ

Balsa disc

Spice tub end

Epoxy lid back
(Hold with masking tape)

Rubber band

Cotton

Notch
for bearing

Release bar here

Parachute cottons

COAST MODE

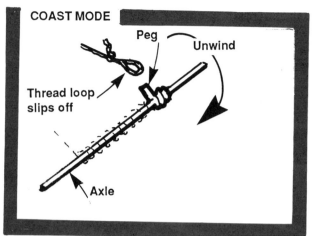

Peg

Unwind

Thread loop slips off

Axle

REVERSE MODE

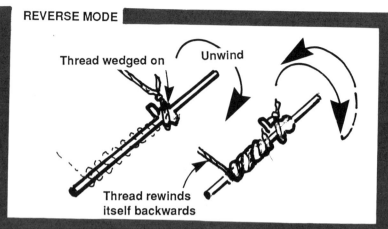

Thread wedged on

Unwind

Thread rewinds itself backwards

PARACHUTE MODE

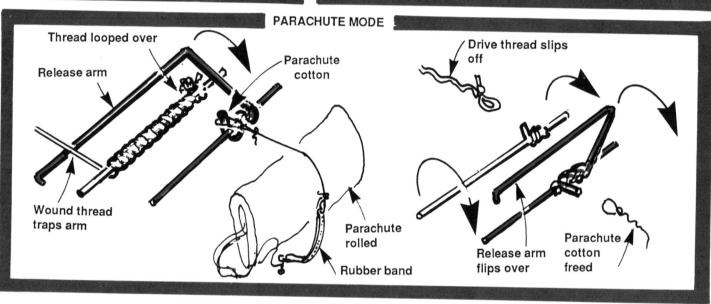

Thread looped over

Release arm

Wound thread traps arm

Parachute cotton

Parachute rolled

Rubber band

Drive thread slips off

Release arm flips over

Parachute cotton freed

6 Robo Buggy

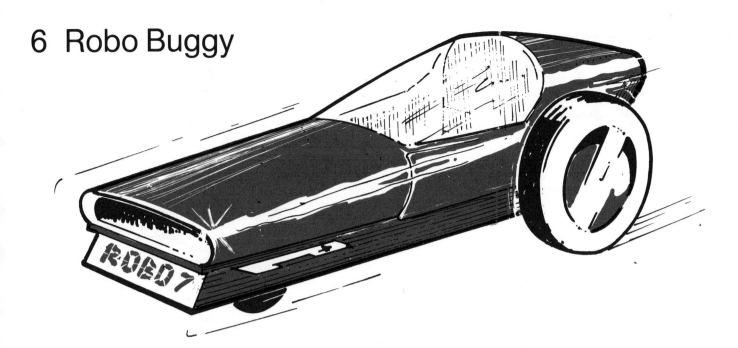

THIS model uses the same principal as the Dragster in achieving reverse but this time the art is in the winding of the cotton on the axle.

Suppose the wheels turn once for every 25 centimetres (10″) travelled. One turn of winding should make it travel that distance either backwards or forwards, depending on which way the wheels are wound. All you need to do to make the buggy go 250 centimetres (100″) forward, reverse 50 (20″) back, then go forward another 75 centimetres (30″) is to wind ten times loop over a peg, a wind or two in the opposite direction, round the peg and three more forward turns again.

A piece of card limits the movement of a castor wheel at the front. Castors, like shopping trolleys, have a mind of their own. The card stops it going too far, with the result that, when in reverse, the car turns, but when going forward it runs straight. The card can be turned over, so that a turn is available in forward, but one of a different radius goes with reverse.

It takes little imagination to see that a card with two notches can give four steering combinations. Add this

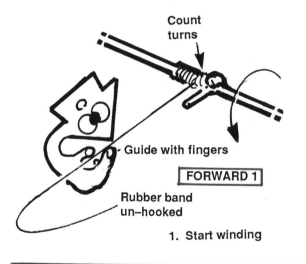

Count turns

Guide with fingers

FORWARD 1

Rubber band un-hooked

1. Start winding

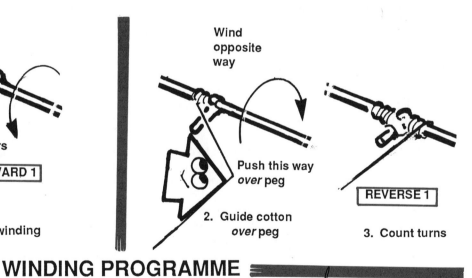

Wind opposite way

Push this way *over* peg

2. Guide cotton *over* peg

REVERSE 1

3. Count turns

WINDING PROGRAMME

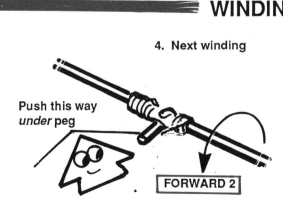

4. Next winding

Push this way *under* peg

FORWARD 2

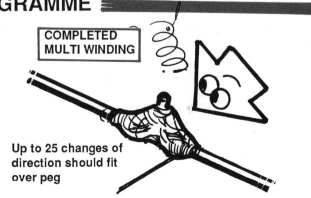

COMPLETED MULTI WINDING

Up to 25 changes of direction should fit over peg

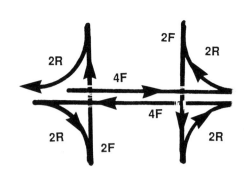

4 turns straight

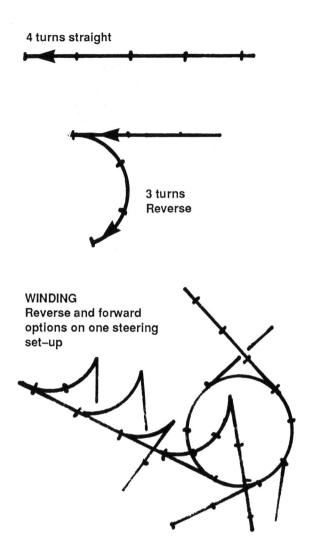

3 turns Reverse

WINDING
Reverse and forward options on one steering set–up

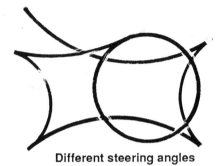

Different steering angles

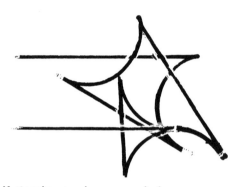

If steering angles are varied unevenly, pattern skews around

WINDING OPTIONS

to the variety of different winds to give a combination of distances and directions and you can see the almost limitless number of permutations. The direction diagrams show just some of the possibilities.

ASSEMBLY
The chassis is a simple box with a hole cut to clear the front castor which is made with a well-fitted wheel bushing so that it does not wobble. Mount it on a vertical wire hinge, so that it turns freely yet does not wobble. This is important, for the castor has to swing in the right direction. It if tilts, the steering will not work. The chassis has a nose-down attitude because large size lids are used for the rear wheels, so check this hinge before adding the bodywork. For the castor

to move freely, there is little weight upon it, yet for it to move at all it needs the grip of a small rubber band used as a tyre. Once this is set up, you can test the buggy.

Only then make and fit the thick paper bodywork. Use paper, not to save weight but to make it easy to form to curves. It will be stiff enough to handle when it has been painted with cellulose or enamel paint.

Once you have mastered the technique of winding and choice of steering plate, the Robo Buggy will steer between obstacles and do three-point turns, wide sweeps and small circles over a course that you have laid out, after setting and remembering the pattern you have chosen.

STEERING OPTIONS

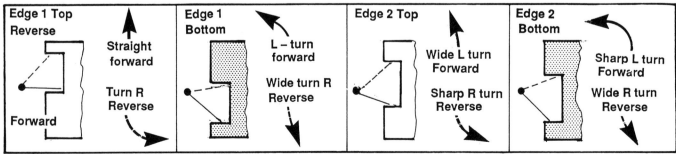

Edge 1 Top Reverse	Edge 1 Bottom	Edge 2 Top	Edge 2 Bottom
Straight forward / Turn R Reverse / Forward	L – turn forward / Wide turn R Reverse	Wide L turn Forward / Sharp R turn Reverse	Sharp L turn Forward / Wide R turn Reverse

ROBO BUGGY PARTS

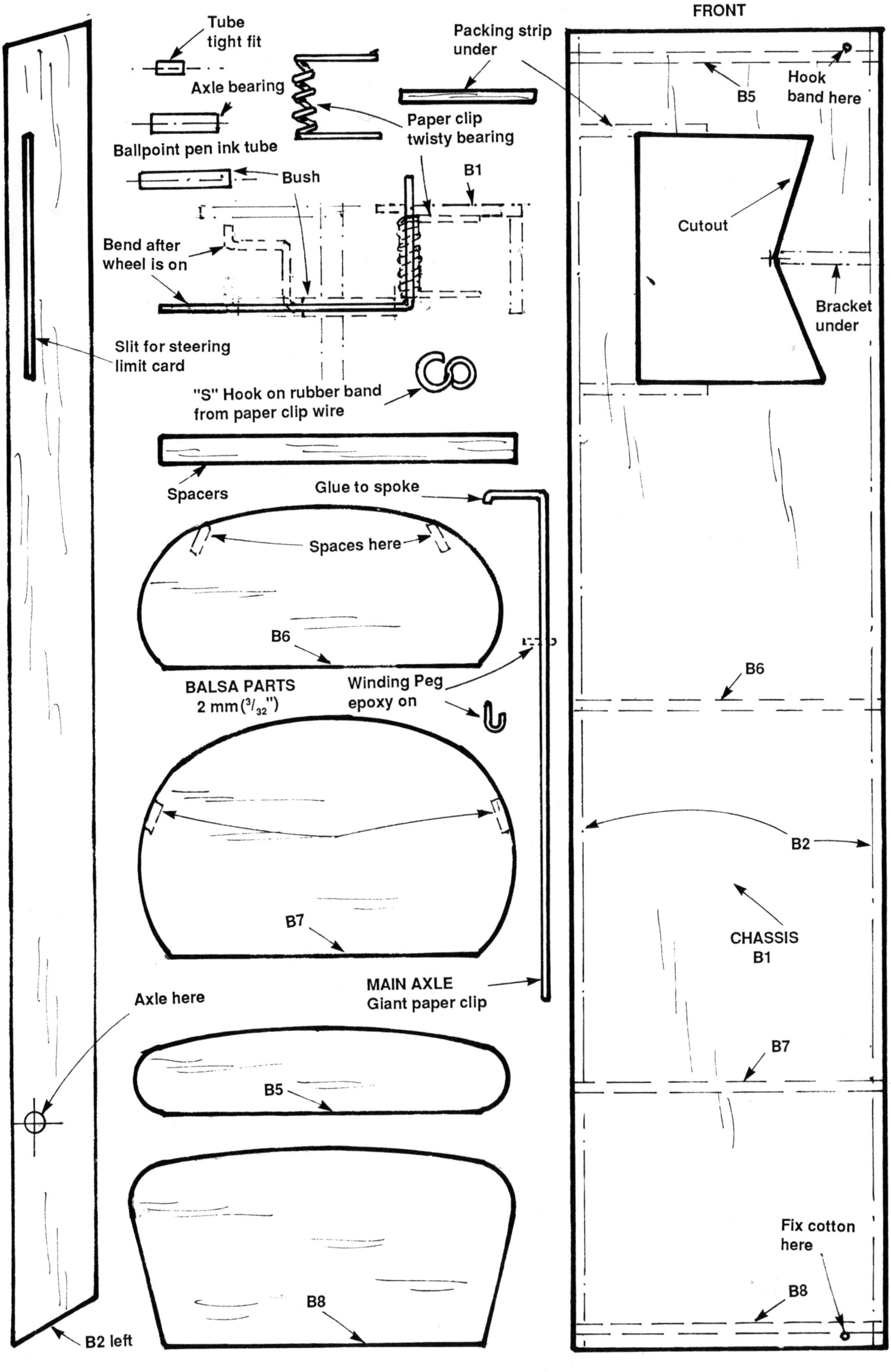

Tube
tight fit

Axle bearing

Ballpoint pen ink tube

Bush

Packing strip
under

Paper clip
twisty bearing

B1

FRONT

B5

Hook
band here

Cutout

Bracket
under

Bend after
wheel is on

Slit for steering
limit card

"S" Hook on rubber band
from paper clip wire

Spacers

Glue to spoke

Spaces here

B6

BALSA PARTS
2 mm (3/32")

Winding Peg
epoxy on

B6

B2

B7

MAIN AXLE
Giant paper clip

CHASSIS
B1

B7

Axle here

B5

Fix cotton
here

B8

B2 left

B8

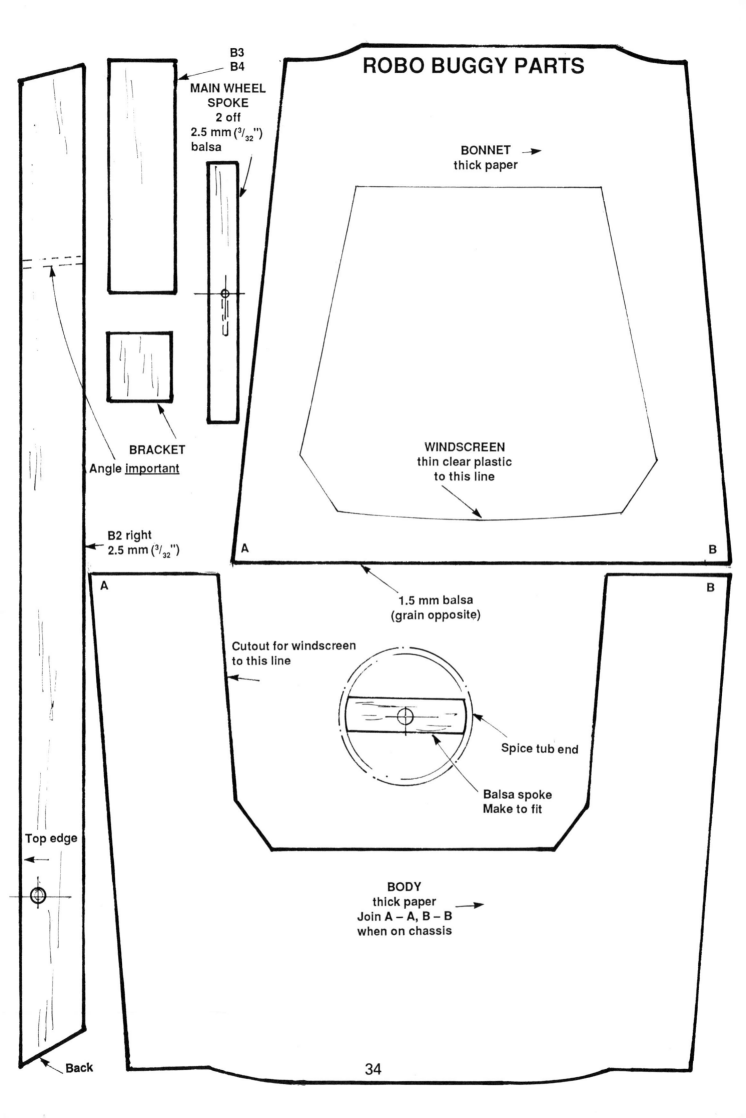

ROBO BUGGY PARTS

B3
B4

MAIN WHEEL
SPOKE
2 off
2.5 mm (³/₃₂")
balsa

BONNET
thick paper →

BRACKET
Angle <u>important</u>

B2 right
2.5 mm (³/₃₂")

WINDSCREEN
thin clear plastic
to this line

A

B

A

B

1.5 mm balsa
(grain opposite)

Cutout for windscreen
to this line

Spice tub end

Balsa spoke
Make to fit

Top edge

BODY
thick paper
Join A – A, B – B
when on chassis

Back

34

ROBO BUGGY ASSEMBLY

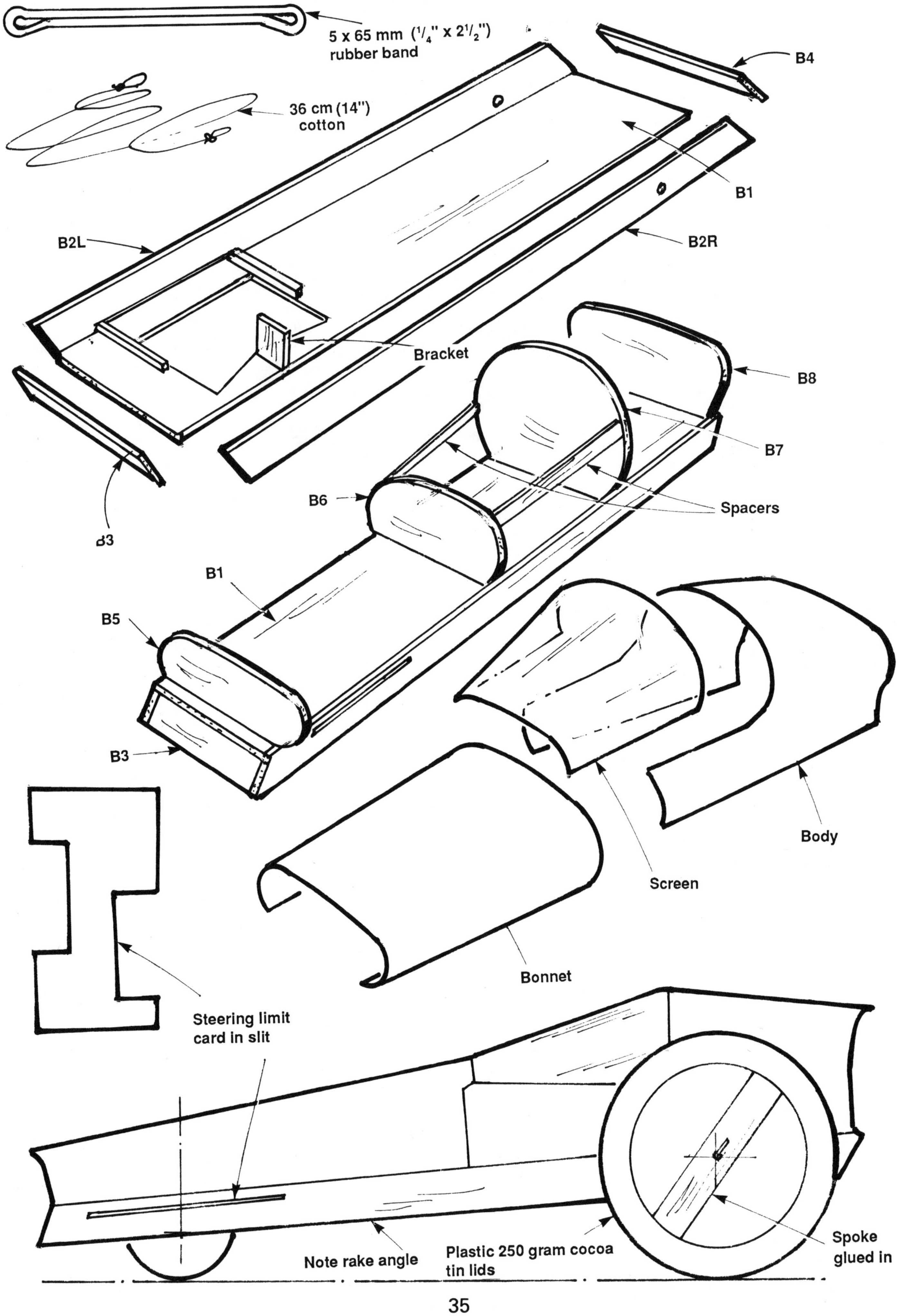

5 x 65 mm ($\frac{1}{4}$" x $2\frac{1}{2}$")
rubber band

36 cm (14")
cotton

B4

B1

B2L

B2R

Bracket

B8

B7

B6

Spacers

B3

B1

B5

B3

Steering limit
card in slit

Screen

Body

Bonnet

Note rake angle

Plastic 250 gram cocoa
tin lids

Spoke
glued in

35

7 Rubber Rower

A twisted rubber band drives the oars of this craft. As the band unwinds, the handle end of the oars goes round in a small circle, but the blades of the oars sweep a larger area (see page 38). A wire double-crank in the centre drives the right-hand oar and the left one has the rubber motor stretched along it. A balsa wood sailor makes steady pulls to drive the craft along, then hurried returns between each stroke.

ASSEMBLY
Cut the hull and sailor from medium grade 2mm (³⁄₃₂″) sheet balsa. The oars are 4mm (³⁄₁₆″) square hard balsa and the blades of the oars are pieces of margarine container plastic. Paper clips and pins form the cranks and bearings. Use waterproof glue and paint the wood to make it waterproof.

The hull is no more than a box, but pre-curve the side pieces slightly. The easiest way of doing this without cracking them is to place them on a soft carpet and roll a tin can along them (see page 38).

You will need epoxy glue to fix the rowlock pivot pins to their brackets and the paper clip guides to the oars. The action has to be smooth, so that the oars move in and out as well as round and round.

The sailor has pins for pivots and tiny reinforcing patches of margarine box plastic, or even sequins, can be epoxied to reduce wear on the arms and hips. Tie the hands with tiny loops of cotton to the ends of the oars, so that the action is free.

Mount the crank wire bearing on an upright paper clip which you can bend to get the best action. Adjust the cranks to make the action free and even. The pull of the fully wound band tries to rock the left hand oar, so a "tweak" to the guide on this side may be needed. Modelling clay weight on the handle of the other oar helps to balance the rubber band.

When adjusted correctly, the oar blades should clear the surface of the water as they start to return.

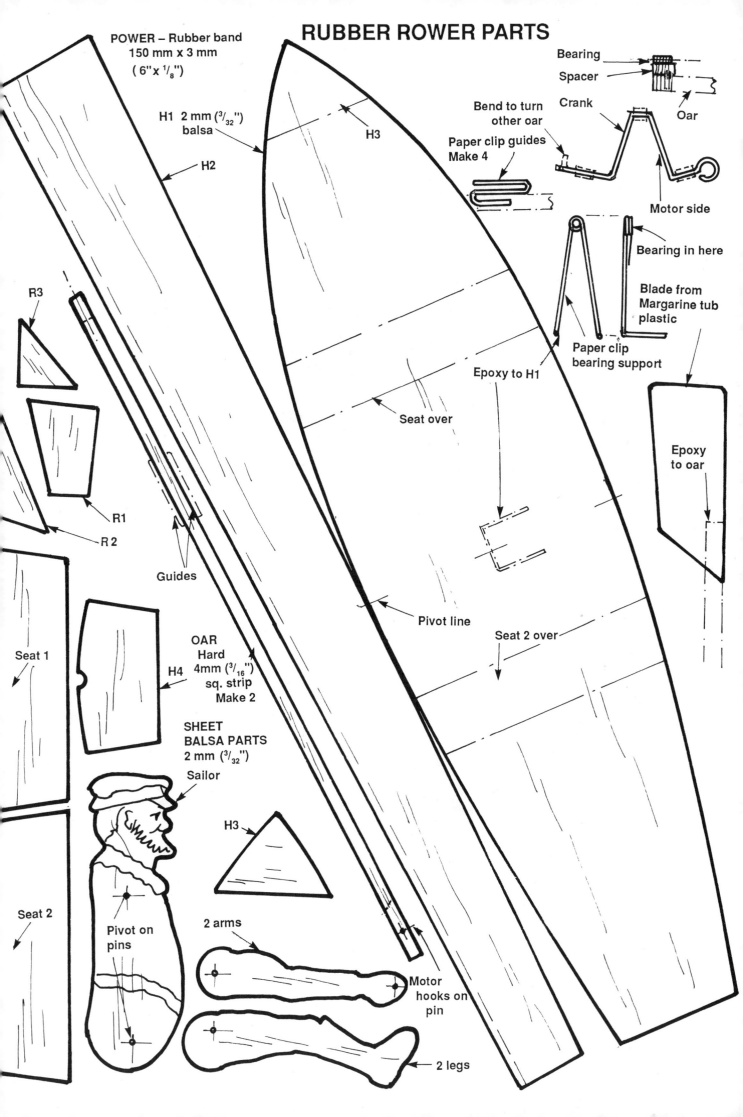

RUBBER ROWER PARTS

POWER – Rubber band
150 mm x 3 mm
(6" x 1/8")

H1 2 mm (3/32")
balsa

H2

H3

Bearing

Spacer

Crank

Oar

Bend to turn
other oar

Paper clip guides
Make 4

Motor side

Bearing in here

Blade from
Margarine tub
plastic

Paper clip
bearing support

Epoxy to H1

Epoxy
to oar

Seat over

Pivot line

Seat 2 over

R3

R1

R 2

Guides

Seat 1

OAR
Hard
4mm (3/16")
sq. strip
Make 2

H4

SHEET
BALSA PARTS
2 mm (3/32")

Sailor

H3

Seat 2

Pivot on
pins

2 arms

Motor
hooks on
pin

2 legs

RUBBER ROWER ASSEMBLY

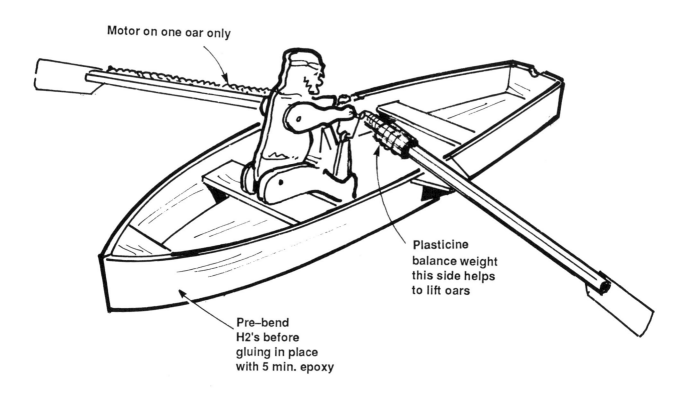

Motor on one oar only

Plasticine
balance weight
this side helps
to lift oars

Pre–bend
H2's before
gluing in place
with 5 min. epoxy

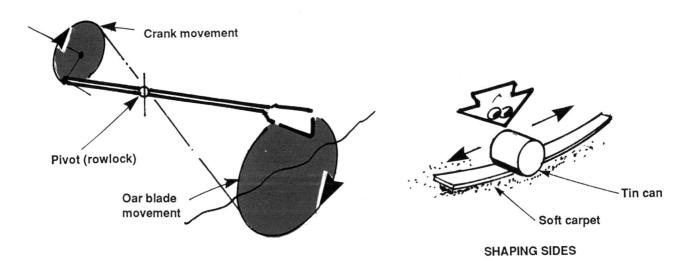

Crank movement

Pivot (rowlock)

Oar blade
movement

Tin can

Soft carpet

SHAPING SIDES

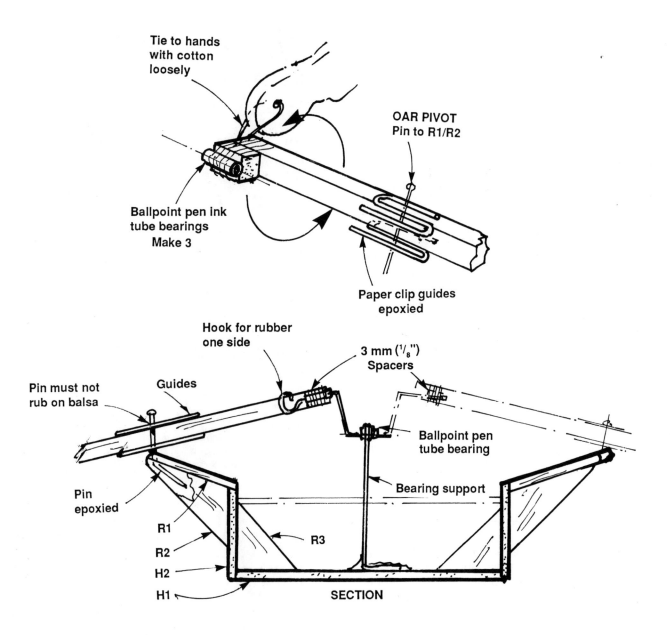

Tie to hands
with cotton
loosely

OAR PIVOT
Pin to R1/R2

Ballpoint pen ink
tube bearings
Make 3

Paper clip guides
epoxied

Hook for rubber
one side

3 mm (⅛")
Spacers

Pin must not
rub on balsa

Guides

Ballpoint pen
tube bearing

Pin
epoxied

Bearing support

R1

R2

R3

H2

H1

SECTION

8 Pogo X2

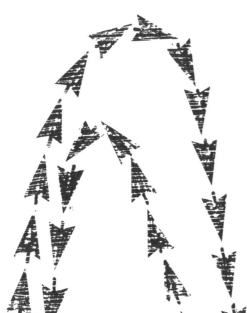

THIS model rocket makes two flights per launch. It carries its own launching system and changes shape as it goes.

Take a look at the sequence diagrams. The model is dropped onto its tail end and a trigger wire is pushed up which unhooks a rubber band. The band drives a rod down the centre of the rocket, pushing against the ground to hurl the rocket skywards. As it takes off, the rod is picked up and carried with it.

There are a set of fins at the bottom of the rod and these slide down as it fires, to become climb stabilisers. At the same time the rubber band unhooks from the rod, but remains captive so that it does not get lost.

The rocket arches over and lands some distance away, nose down. As it hits the ground, a second trigger system operates, releasing another rubber band which drives the rod in the opposite direction. Up goes the rocket, but in a different shape this time because the fins are now close to the body. This gives the rocket quite a different flight path. It comes back towards the first launch area, but floats down sideways and lands more softly.

ASSEMBLY

Use hard balsa wood strips for the rocket body and rod: 5mm (¼″) square for the former and 4mm (³⁄₁₆″) square for the rod. Small pieces of 1.5mm (¹⁄₁₆″) sheet brace the nose and tail ends. Cut the fins from a cheese spread box. Paper clip wire forms the trigger arms and the trigger pushrods are 20 s.w.g. piano wire. Scraps of cotton bud stem form the bearing and guide tubes, all epoxied securely in place.

There is a sudden release of power in this model. So the angles of the release hooks and those on the rod have to be set right. Those bands slip from one to the other to "fire". For safety reasons, a piece of hard foam plastic (draught excluder strip) is glued around the nose end of the rod. This is a fierce little model, so stand well clear and lean it away from you slightly. Do not point it at people, and use it on a calm day. Be careful not to move the release trigger wires after hooking the rubber bands in place.

FLYING THE POGO X2

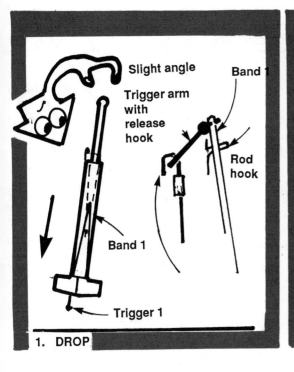

Slight angle

Trigger arm with release hook

Band 1

Rod hook

Band 1

Trigger 1

1. DROP

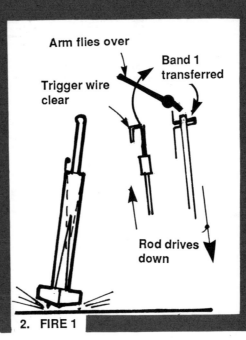

Arm flies over

Band 1 transferred

Trigger wire clear

Rod drives down

2. FIRE 1

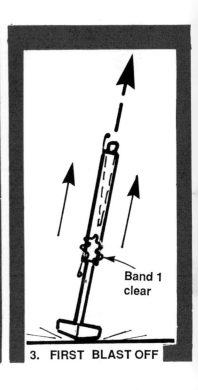

Band 1 clear

3. FIRST BLAST OFF

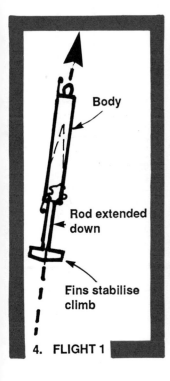

Body

Rod extended down

Fins stabilise climb

4. FLIGHT 1

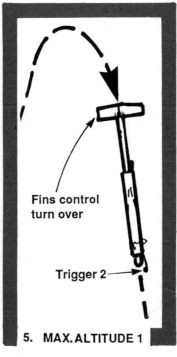

Fins control turn over

Trigger 2

5. MAX. ALTITUDE 1

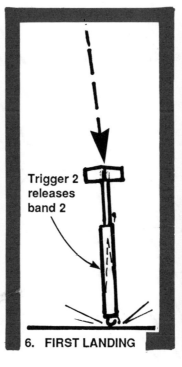

Trigger 2 releases band 2

6. FIRST LANDING

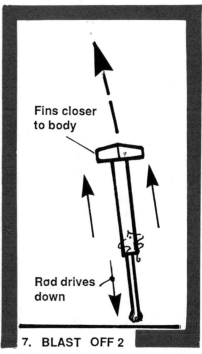

Fins closer to body

Rod drives down

7. BLAST OFF 2

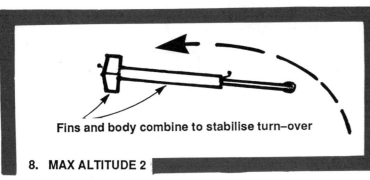

Fins and body combine to stabilise turn–over

8. MAX ALTITUDE 2

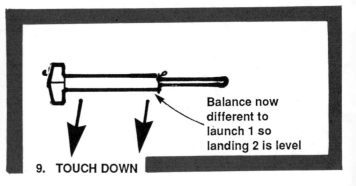

Balance now different to launch 1 so landing 2 is level

9. TOUCH DOWN

POGO X2 PARTS

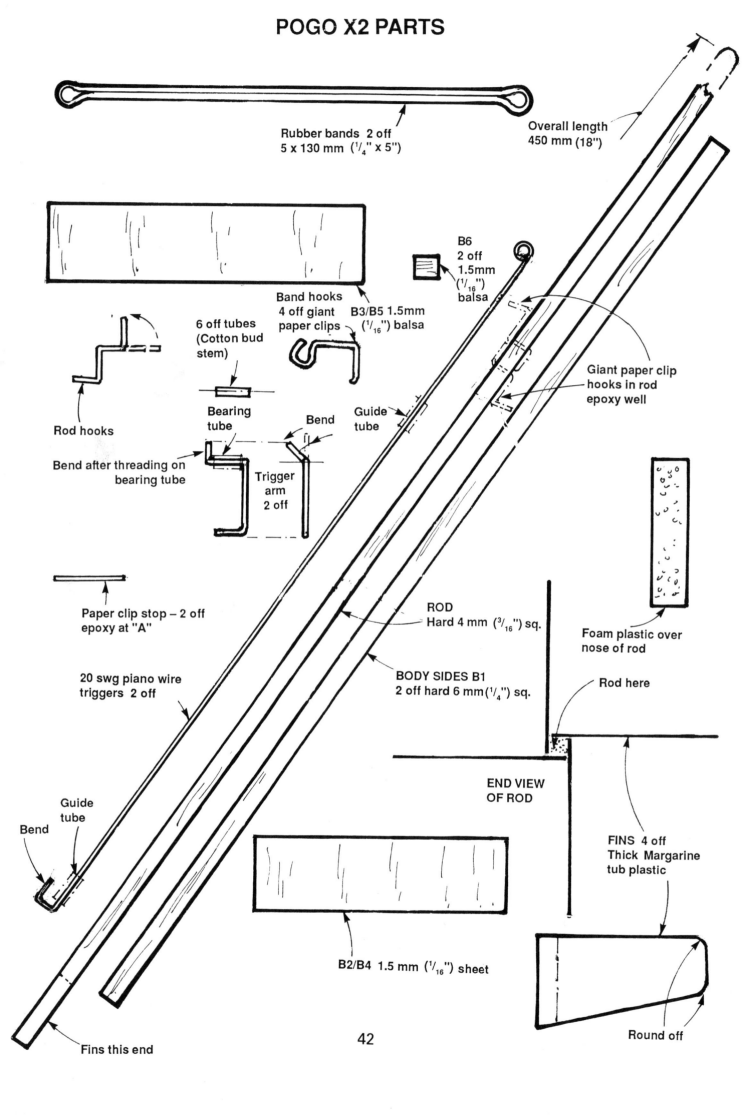

Rubber bands 2 off
5 x 130 mm ($\frac{1}{4}$" x 5")

Overall length
450 mm (18")

B6
2 off
1.5mm
($\frac{1}{16}$")
balsa

Band hooks
4 off giant
paper clips

B3/B5 1.5mm
($\frac{1}{16}$") balsa

6 off tubes
(Cotton bud
stem)

Rod hooks

Bearing
tube

Bend

Guide
tube

Giant paper clip
hooks in rod
epoxy well

Bend after threading on
bearing tube

Trigger
arm
2 off

Paper clip stop – 2 off
epoxy at "A"

ROD
Hard 4 mm ($\frac{3}{16}$") sq.

Foam plastic over
nose of rod

20 swg piano wire
triggers 2 off

BODY SIDES B1
2 off hard 6 mm ($\frac{1}{4}$") sq.

Rod here

END VIEW
OF ROD

FINS 4 off
Thick Margarine
tub plastic

Guide
tube

Bend

B2/B4 1.5 mm ($\frac{1}{16}$") sheet

Round off

Fins this end

42

POGO X2 ASSEMBLY

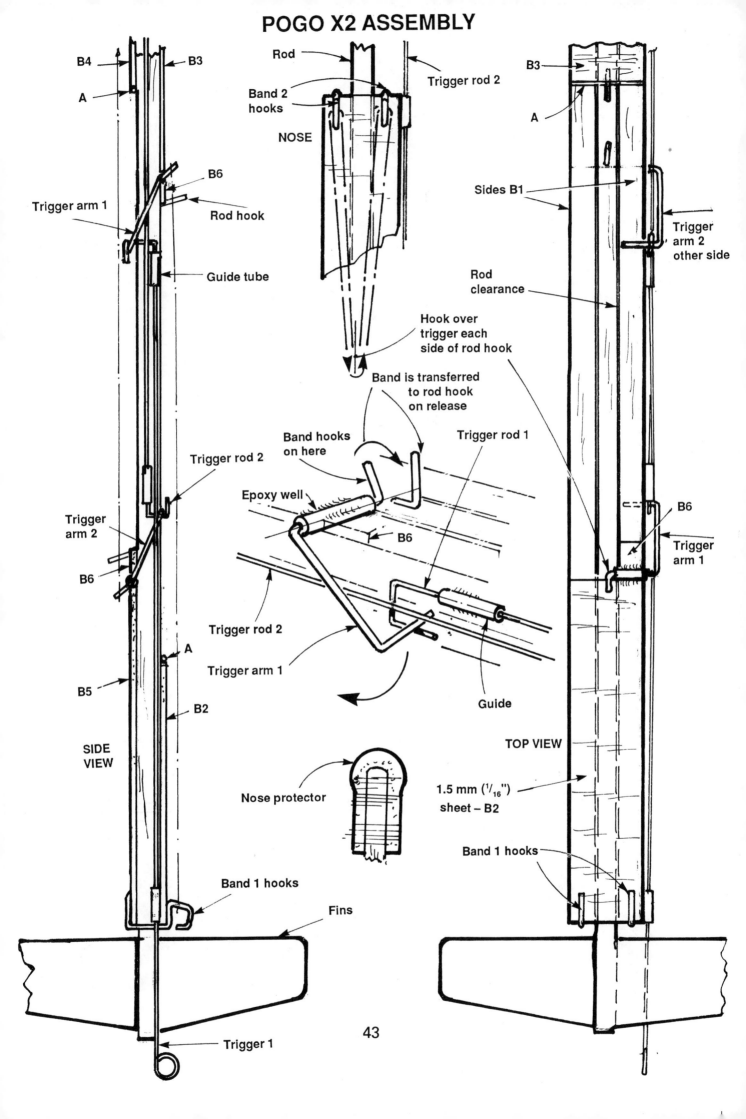

B4

B3

A

Rod

Trigger rod 2

Band 2 hooks

NOSE

B3

A

Trigger arm 1

B6

Rod hook

Sides B1

Guide tube

Trigger arm 2 other side

Rod clearance

Hook over trigger each side of rod hook

Band is transferred to rod hook on release

Trigger rod 2

Band hooks on here

Trigger rod 1

Trigger arm 2

Epoxy well

B6

B6

B6

Trigger arm 1

Trigger rod 2

Trigger arm 1

B5

A

Guide

B2

TOP VIEW

SIDE VIEW

Nose protector

1.5 mm ($^1/_{16}$") sheet – B2

Band 1 hooks

Band 1 hooks

Fins

Trigger 1

9 Frog

A strong rubber band unwinds thread from a shaft which has a crank at one end and, at the other, a release arm which is held by a trigger. When the Frog is dropped on the ground, the crank is released to make one complete turn. This drives a thrust rod onto the ground, hurling the model up and forward.

The model is mostly expanded polystyrene, so is light and even tries to glide. It pancakes on its large front legs, then rocks back to leap up again. The sequence of jumping is shown on the drawings.

ASSEMBLY

Use hard grade balsa wood for the mechanism. The rest is wire bending, remembering to use giant size paper clip wire for the shaft. Make a slight dent in the shaft with pliers where the thread attachment hook has to be epoxied. There is a very strong pull from the rubber bands so, if it is not secure, the thread will slip.

Experiment with the angles of the top of the release end of the crank wire and the amount of overlap made on it by the trigger. Aim to get a "hair trigger" effect, so that it "fires" at the least jog as the frog sits down, yet not so close as to skip past when fully wound.

All this is easier to see when the model is complete. The sequence sketches on page 48 show how to "trim" its bouncing path.

FROG ACTION SEQUENCE

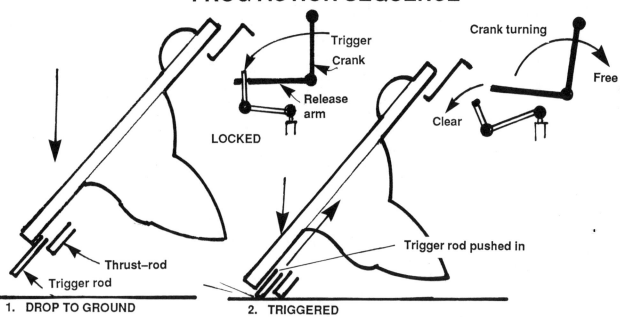

Trigger
Crank
Release arm
LOCKED

Crank turning
Free
Clear

Thrust-rod
Trigger rod
Trigger rod pushed in

1. DROP TO GROUND

2. TRIGGERED

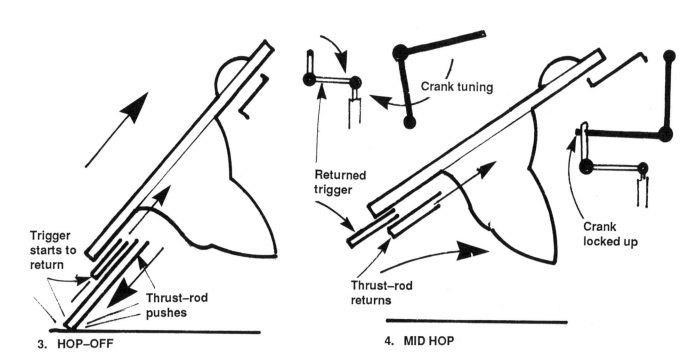

Crank tuning

Returned trigger

Crank locked up

Trigger starts to return

Thrust-rod pushes

Thrust-rod returns

3. HOP-OFF

4. MID HOP

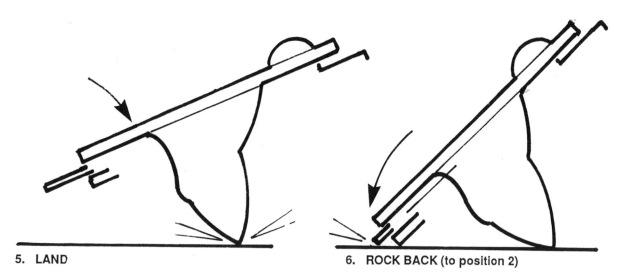

5. LAND

6. ROCK BACK (to position 2)

FROG PARTS

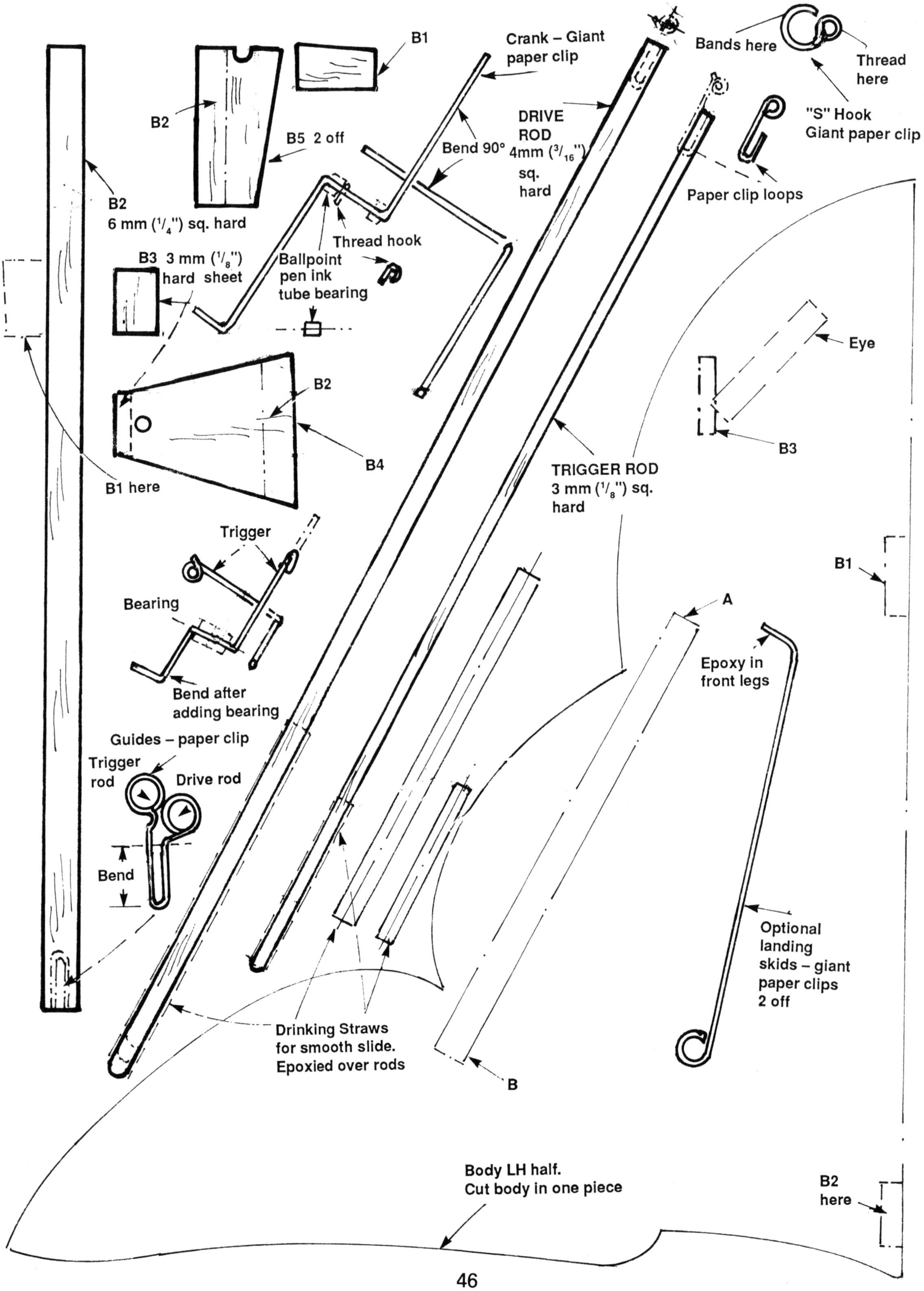

B1

B2

B5 2 off

B2
6 mm ($\frac{1}{4}$") sq. hard

B3 3 mm ($\frac{1}{8}$") hard sheet

Thread hook

Ballpoint pen ink tube bearing

B2

B4

B1 here

Trigger

Bearing

Bend after adding bearing

Guides – paper clip

Trigger rod

Drive rod

Bend

Crank – Giant paper clip

Bend 90°

DRIVE ROD
4mm ($\frac{3}{16}$") sq. hard

Bands here

Thread here

"S" Hook
Giant paper clip

Paper clip loops

TRIGGER ROD
3 mm ($\frac{1}{8}$") sq. hard

Eye

B3

B1

A

Epoxy in front legs

Optional landing skids – giant paper clips 2 off

Drinking Straws for smooth slide. Epoxied over rods

B

Body LH half.
Cut body in one piece

B2 here

FROG PARTS

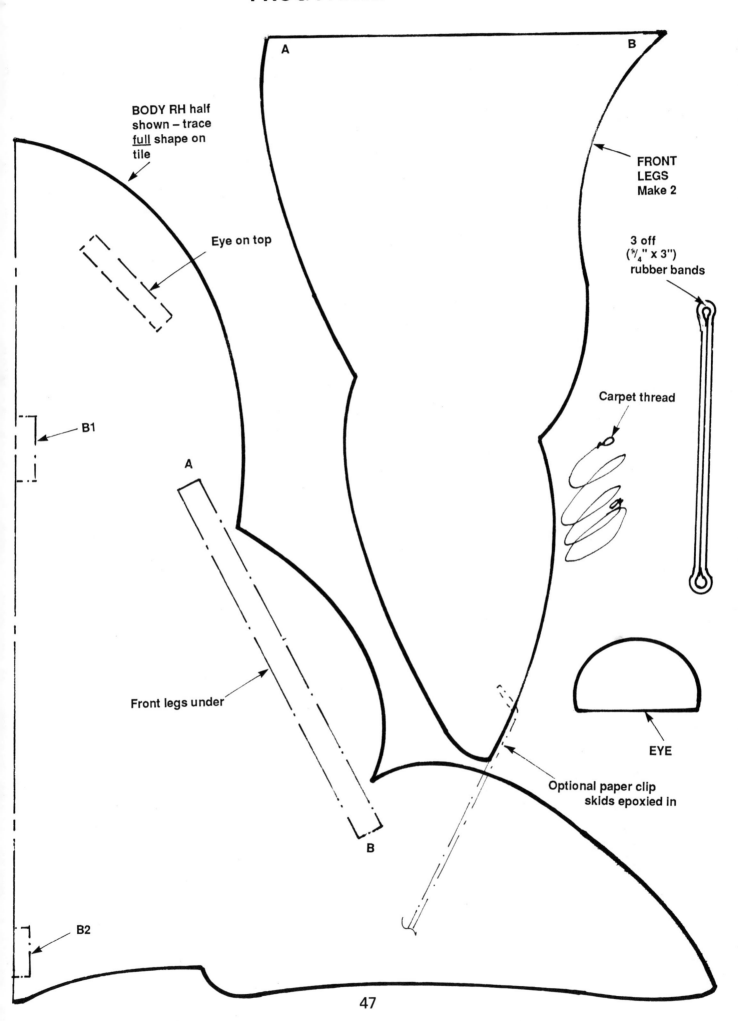

A

B

BODY RH half shown – trace <u>full</u> shape on tile

FRONT LEGS Make 2

Eye on top

3 off (³/₄" x 3") rubber bands

B1

Carpet thread

A

Front legs under

EYE

B

Optional paper clip skids epoxied in

B2

FROG TESTING

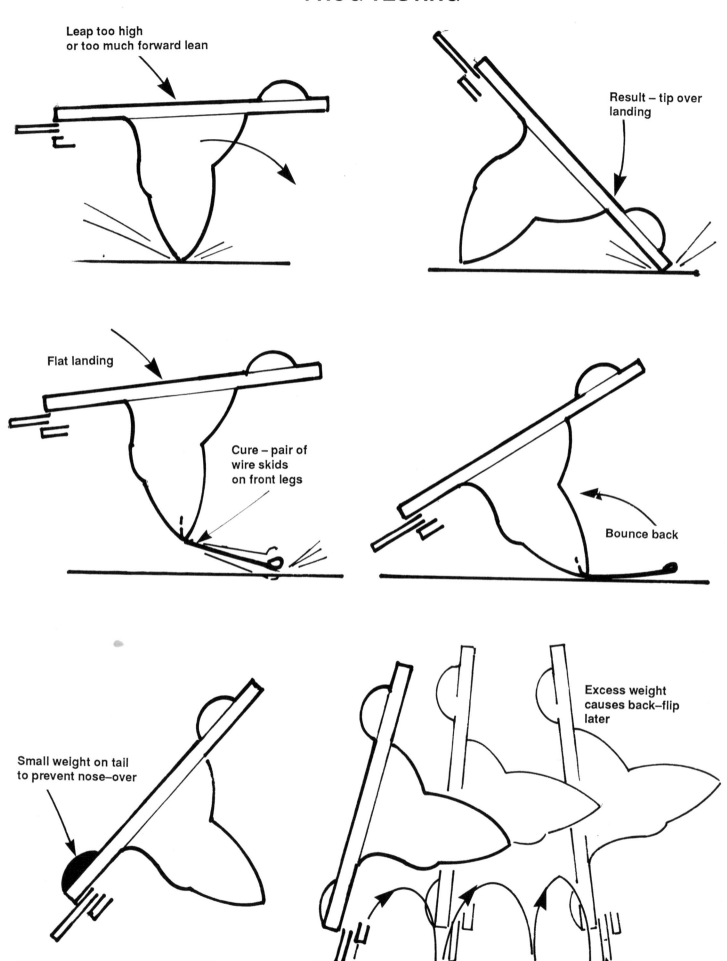

FROG ASSEMBLY

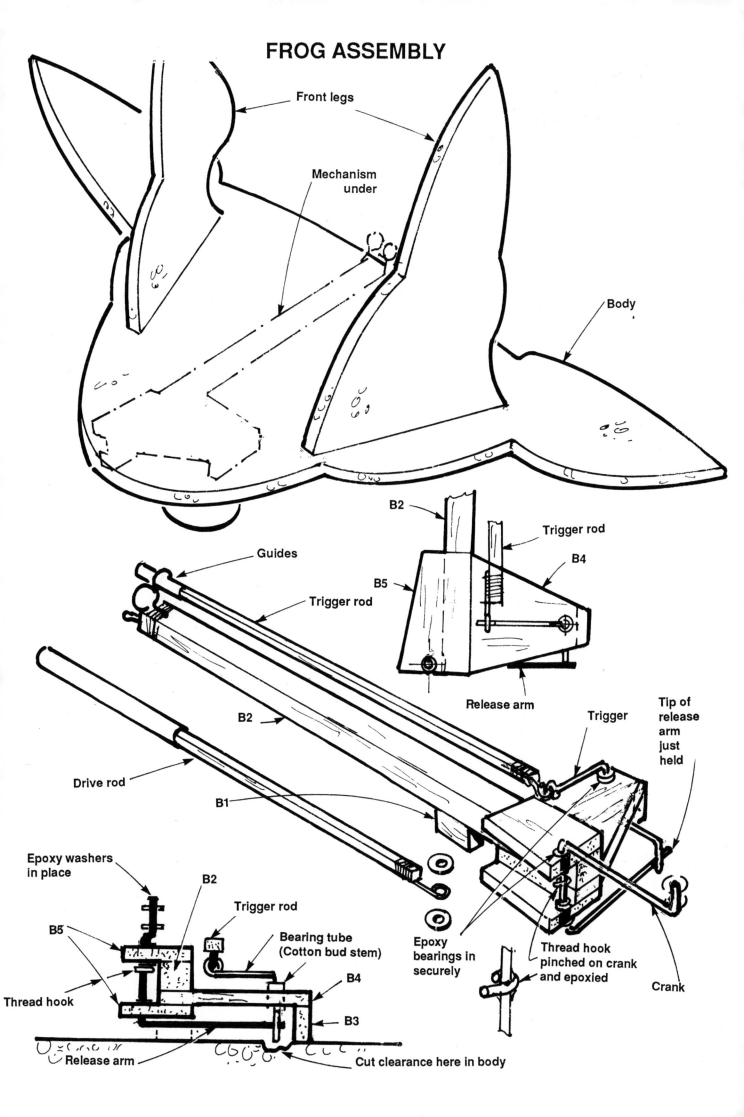

Front legs

Mechanism under

Body

B2

Trigger rod

B5

B4

Release arm

Guides

Trigger rod

B2

Drive rod

B1

Trigger

Tip of release arm just held

Epoxy bearings in securely

Thread hook pinched on crank and epoxied

Crank

Epoxy washers in place

B2

Trigger rod

Bearing tube (Cotton bud stem)

B5

B4

Thread hook

B3

Release arm

Cut clearance here in body

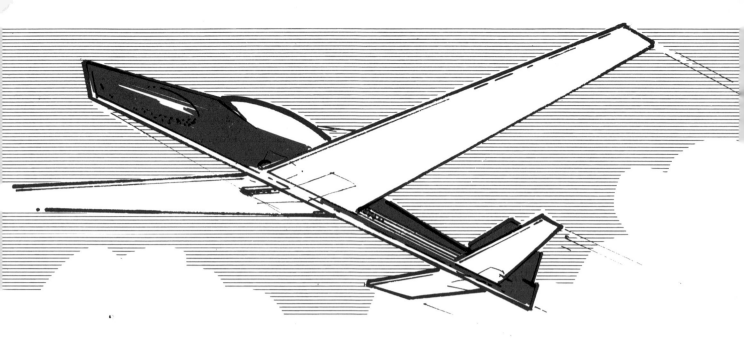

10 Jump Jet

JUMP Jet rises vertically with its fuselage horizontal, ready to go into transition flight. A "booster" carries it up and, when the booster slows down, the wings, which have been folded downwards in "stabiliser mode", spring into "flight mode".

Then a second catapult, pushing against the mass of the booster, hurls the aircraft into a fast horizontal flight path. All that holds the model onto the launch "booster" is air pressure, and all that stops the second catapult firing is the position of the wings at lift-off.

ASSEMBLY

Join the wings and tail halves together, so that the pair on each side of the fuselage fold down together. Make

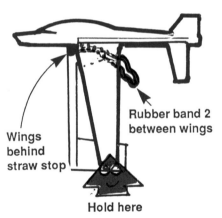

Wings behind straw stop

Rubber band 2 between wings

Hold here

1. PRE–LAUNCH

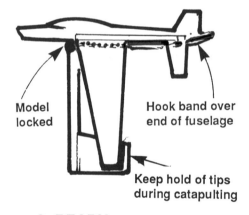

Model locked

Hook band over end of fuselage

Keep hold of tips during catapulting

2. READY

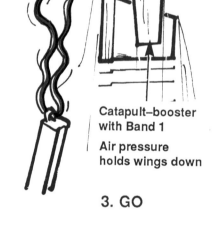

Catapult–booster with Band 1

Air pressure holds wings down

3. GO

JUMP JET FLIGHT SEQUENCE

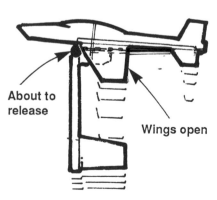

About to release

Wings open

4. MAX. BOOST ALTITUDE

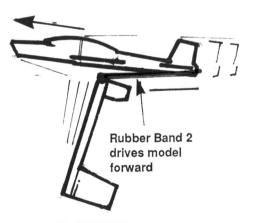

Rubber Band 2 drives model forward

5. TRANSITION

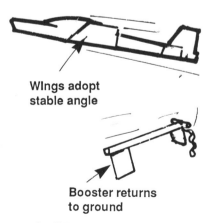

Wings adopt stable angle

Booster returns to ground

6. GLIDE

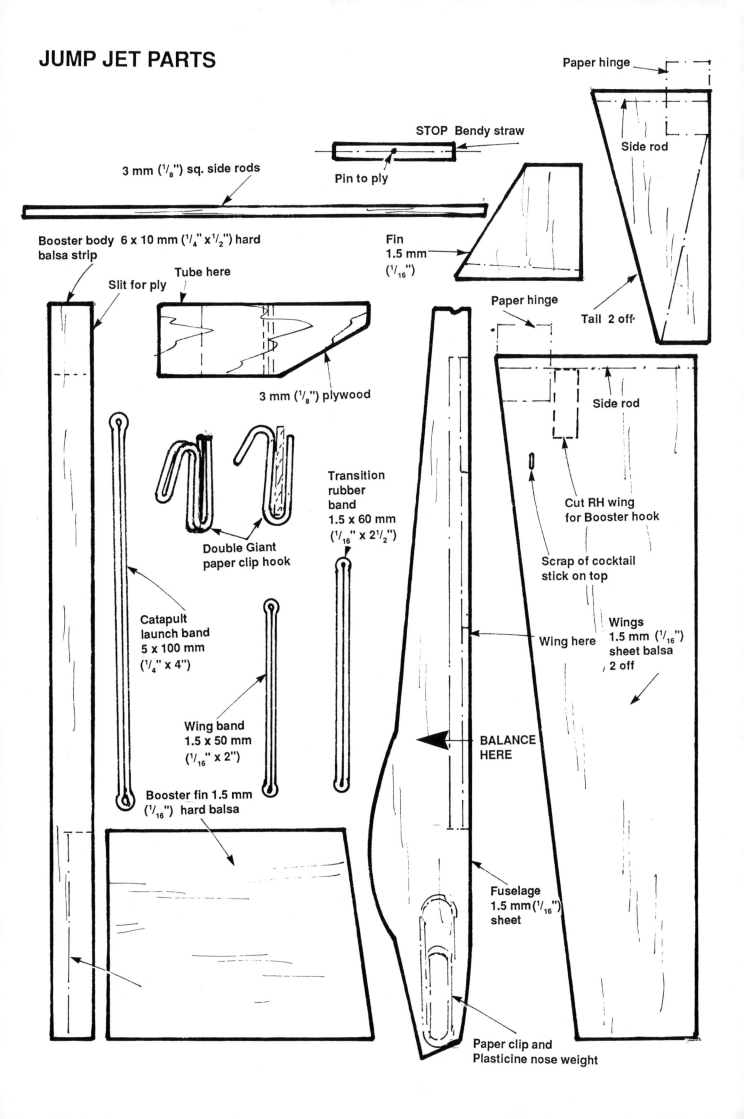

JUMP JET PARTS

3 mm (¹/₈") sq. side rods

STOP Bendy straw

Pin to ply

Paper hinge

Side rod

Booster body 6 x 10 mm (¹/₄" x¹/₂") hard balsa strip

Slit for ply

Tube here

Fin 1.5 mm (¹/₁₆")

Paper hinge

Tail 2 off

3 mm (¹/₈") plywood

Side rod

Double Giant paper clip hook

Transition rubber band 1.5 x 60 mm (¹/₁₆" x 2¹/₂")

Cut RH wing for Booster hook

Scrap of cocktail stick on top

Catapult launch band 5 x 100 mm (¹/₄" x 4")

Wings 1.5 mm (¹/₁₆") sheet balsa 2 off

Wing band 1.5 x 50 mm (¹/₁₆" x 2")

Wing here

BALANCE HERE

Booster fin 1.5 mm (¹/₁₆") hard balsa

Fuselage 1.5 mm (¹/₁₆") sheet

Paper clip and Plasticine nose weight

JUMP JET ASSEMBLY

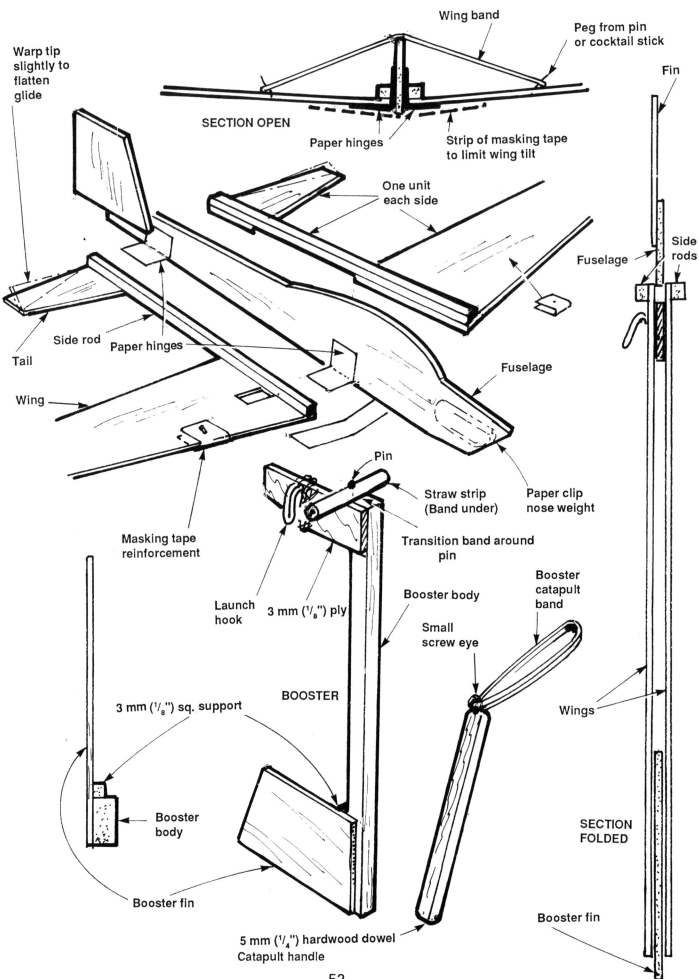

Wing band

Peg from pin
or cocktail stick

Fin

Warp tip
slightly to
flatten
glide

SECTION OPEN

Paper hinges

Strip of masking tape
to limit wing tilt

One unit
each side

Side rods

Fuselage

Side rod   Paper hinges

Tail

Fuselage

Wing

Paper clip
nose weight

Masking tape
reinforcement

Pin

Straw strip
(Band under)

Transition band around
pin

Booster
catapult
band

Launch
hook

3 mm (¹/₈") ply

Booster body

Small
screw eye

Wings

3 mm (¹/₈") sq. support

BOOSTER

Booster
body

SECTION
FOLDED

Booster fin

Booster fin

5 mm (¹/₄") hardwood dowel
Catapult handle

52

the hinges from folded writing paper; flex them several times before gluing in place. Make sure that the 3mm (⅛") square strips are level with each other and not higher at one end than at the other, as this will cause the model to flip over and spiral down.

A very weak rubber band pulls the wings up and tilts the tips up to give stable flight. The front of the wings, near the fuselage, presses against a piece of thick drinking straw (bendy straw type). This holds the model in place while the second rubber band is hooked over the tail end of the fuselage.

Booster

Hard balsa is used here and comes in for some punishment. A scrap of 3mm (⅛") plywood at the top forms a seat for the model. It also carries a double paper clip hook to enable it to be launched by hand catapult. That hook fits through a slot in the wing of the model. Experiment by adding weights in the form of nails, bound with masking tape to the bottom edge of that ply plate. The heavier the weight, the higher it can be catapulted, up to a point, that is, as then it becomes unstable and falls about before the model fires off.

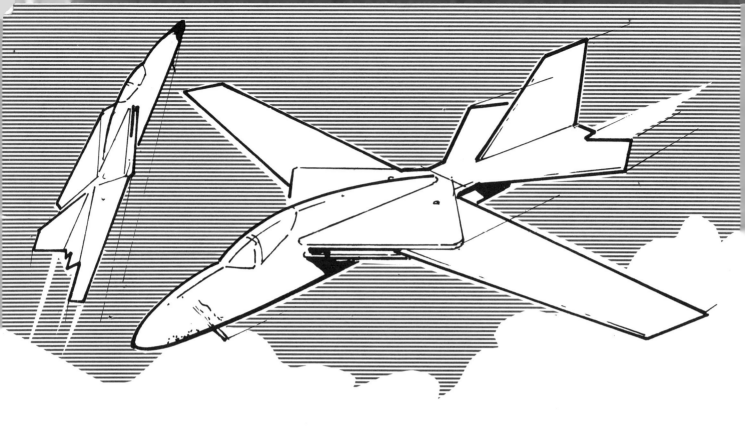

11 F1-11 Swing Wing

THIS is a catapult glider model with a difference. Whereas the wings might have been made to blow back, these are restrained by a simple time delay device. The degree of delay can be set before flight and is quite independent of how fast or at what angle the model is catapulted.

When the model speeds away in a climb with folded wings, the delay unit starts to open the wings gradually so that the model does not suddenly jerk into a stall or loop. It is also possible to catapult the F1-11 with wings partly folded, or with fully open wings to start the flight.

ASSEMBLY
The timing device is a kinked paper clip inside a small piece of silicon rubber tube. You can find this tube at model aeroplane shops and it is normally used as a fuel pipe. Be sure to buy silicone rubber, not neoprene or black rubber tube, as silicone has the right stretch and is capable of gripping the paper clip tightly, until it has relaxed. With the correct pull from the rubber band, it will move evenly.

Trial and error will determine how fast it should move. Once adjusted, it is only necessary to slide the wings back by hand, then slide the wire back. Hold the wire with the fingers that grip the model as it is launched. Weaker bands or a larger kink in the clip wire slow it down; stronger bands or a small kink speed it up. Aim at about five seconds delay for a start.

F1–11 SETTING

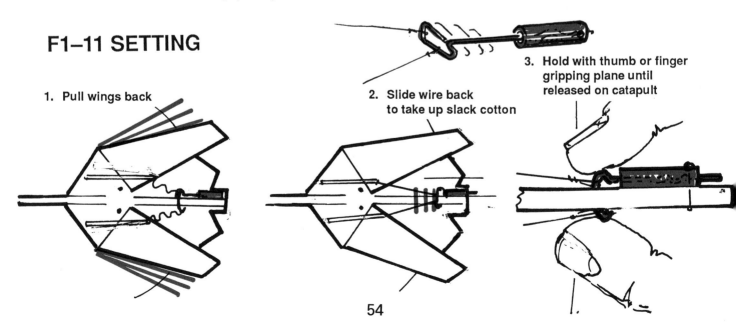

1. **Pull wings back**

2. **Slide wire back to take up slack cotton**

3. **Hold with thumb or finger gripping plane until released on catapult**

54

F1–11 PARTS

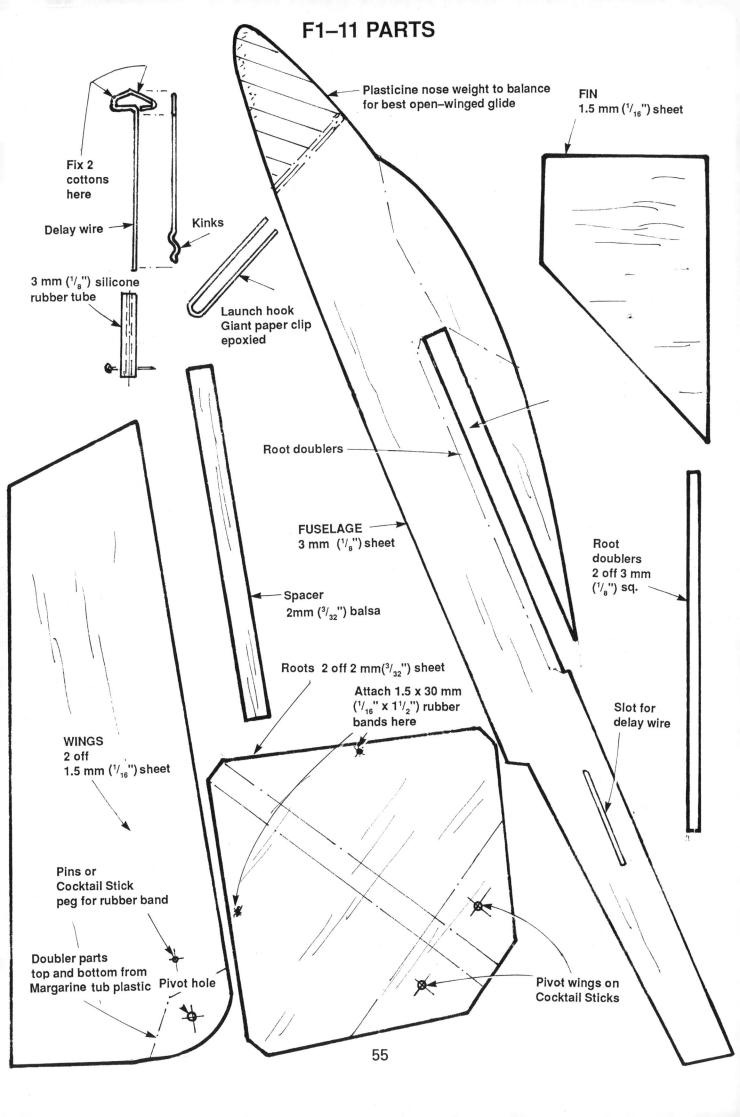

Fix 2 cottons here

Delay wire

Kinks

3 mm (¹/₈") silicone rubber tube

Launch hook
Giant paper clip
epoxied

Plasticine nose weight to balance
for best open–winged glide

FIN
1.5 mm (¹/₁₆") sheet

Root doublers

FUSELAGE
3 mm (¹/₈") sheet

Root
doublers
2 off 3 mm
(¹/₈") sq.

Spacer
2mm (³/₃₂") balsa

Roots 2 off 2 mm(³/₃₂") sheet

Attach 1.5 x 30 mm
(¹/₁₆" x 1¹/₂") rubber
bands here

Slot for
delay wire

WINGS
2 off
1.5 mm (¹/₁₆") sheet

Pins or
Cocktail Stick
peg for rubber band

Doubler parts
top and bottom from
Margarine tub plastic

Pivot hole

Pivot wings on
Cocktail Sticks

55

F1–11 ASSEMBLY AND TAIL

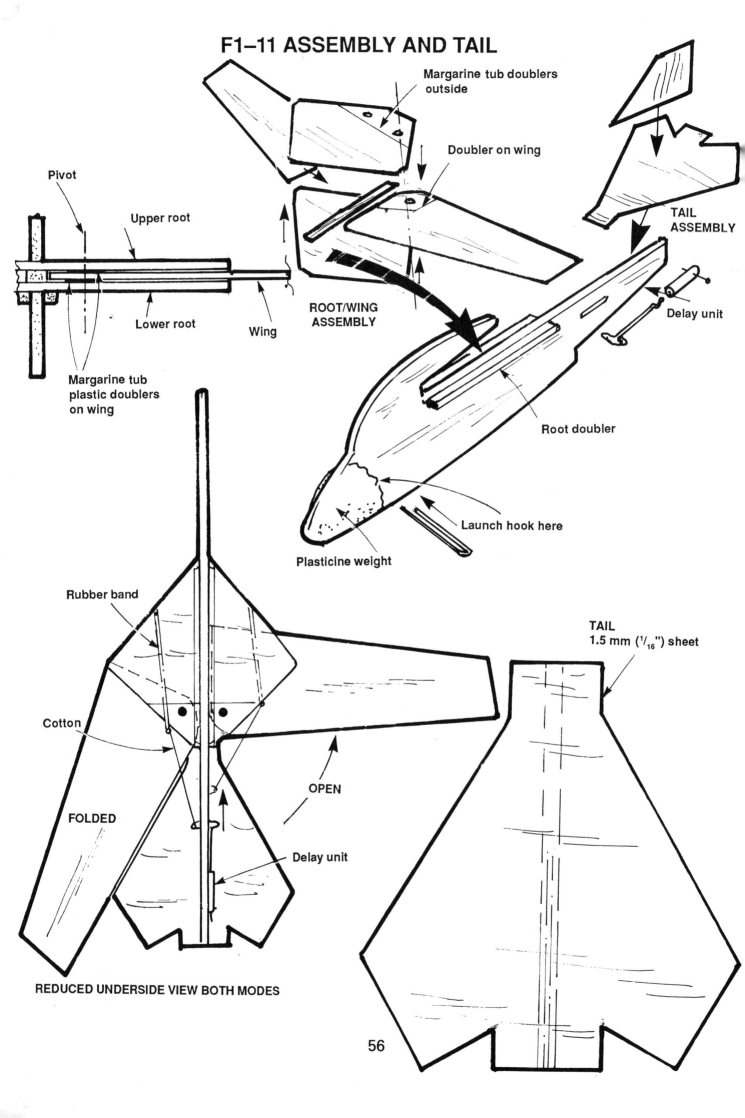

Pivot

Upper root

Lower root

Wing

Margarine tub plastic doublers on wing

Margarine tub doublers outside

Doubler on wing

ROOT/WING ASSEMBLY

TAIL ASSEMBLY

Delay unit

Root doubler

Launch hook here

Plasticine weight

Rubber band

Cotton

FOLDED

OPEN

Delay unit

REDUCED UNDERSIDE VIEW BOTH MODES

TAIL
1.5 mm ($^1/_{16}$") sheet

12 Salamander

THIS racing canoe has paddles that drive with real power.

Look at the sketch sequence on page 61. See how the position of the pivots on the paddles and arms combine with the sweep of the crank that drives them. Notice how the paddle blades go into the water at an angle to slip down without slowing the craft as it speeds along. See the long sweep of the paddle as it drives against the water and watch how quickly the blade leaves the water to return for the next stroke. That's why the Salamander is a racer.

The power comes from a simple rubber band pulling cotton wound on a paper clip wire shaft across the hull. The cotton is looped through an "S" hook in the manner of the Wheeler, to give a good long run.

ASSEMBLY

Balsa wood is used extensively in this model. Use medium grade 2mm (³⁄₃₂″) sheet for the hull bottom and 1.5mm (¹⁄₁₆″) for the sides, seat, bulkheads and Indians. 6mm (¼″) scrap strip forms the paddle handles and a couple of spacers on the Indians' shoulders.

Slide the bearing tube onto the crank wire before bending it to shape. If the tubes (ink tube or cotton bud sticks) are a little loose, the pull of the driving cotton should prevent the wire wobbling.

Pins form the arm pivots. There is not really any need to bush the holes, just fix a sequin to the wood with epoxy glue before piercing it, then wiggle the pin for a free action.

Remember that this is a boat. Use a water-resistant type of PVA glue or make quite sure that it is hardened (two or three days) and paint or varnish over it.

Use plastic cut from the thinnest lid of an empty margarine tub for the paddle blades. Balsa blades try to float, so slowing down the action. The paper-thin, springy plastic is just the job.

Always use the recommended size of rubber band to drive your Salamander – stronger bands will bend the shaft, a thicker shaft will not turn so many times per stretch, or a weaker band will not give so lively a performance.

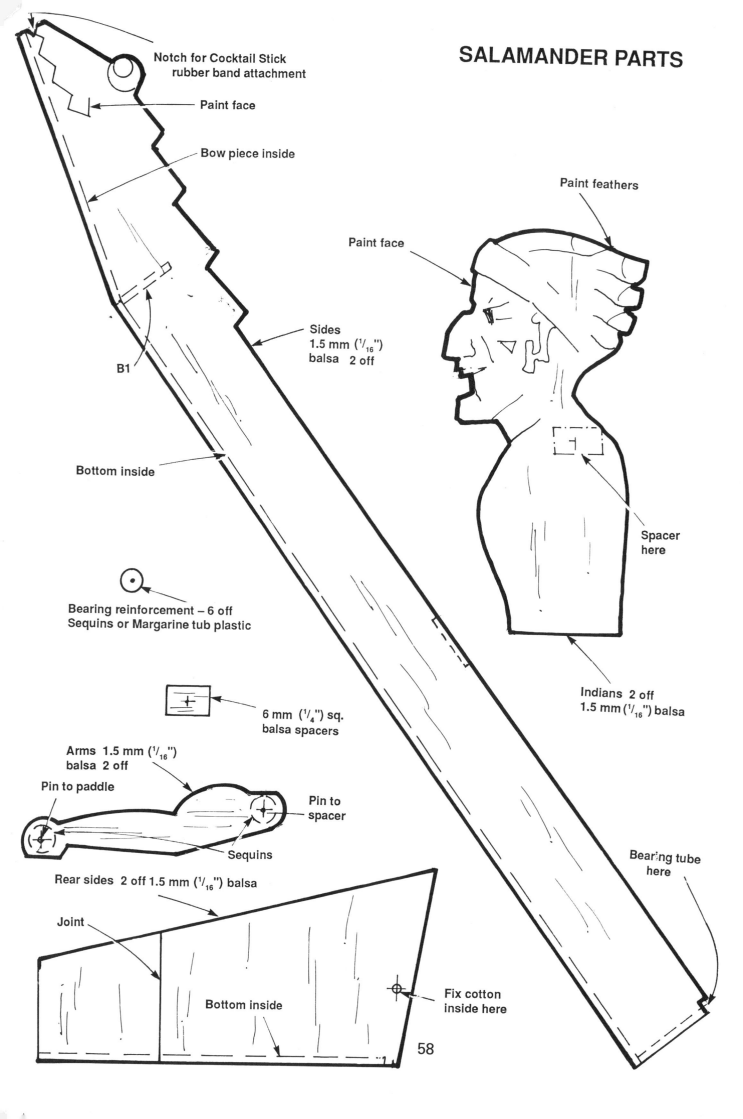

SALAMANDER PARTS

Notch for Cocktail Stick
rubber band attachment

Paint face

Bow piece inside

Paint feathers

Paint face

Sides
1.5 mm ($^1/_{16}$")
balsa 2 off

B1

Bottom inside

Spacer
here

Bearing reinforcement – 6 off
Sequins or Margarine tub plastic

Indians 2 off
1.5 mm ($^1/_{16}$") balsa

6 mm ($^1/_4$") sq.
balsa spacers

Arms 1.5 mm ($^1/_{16}$")
balsa 2 off

Pin to paddle

Pin to
spacer

Sequins

Bearing tube
here

Rear sides 2 off 1.5 mm ($^1/_{16}$") balsa

Joint

Bottom inside

Fix cotton
inside here

58

SALAMANDER PARTS

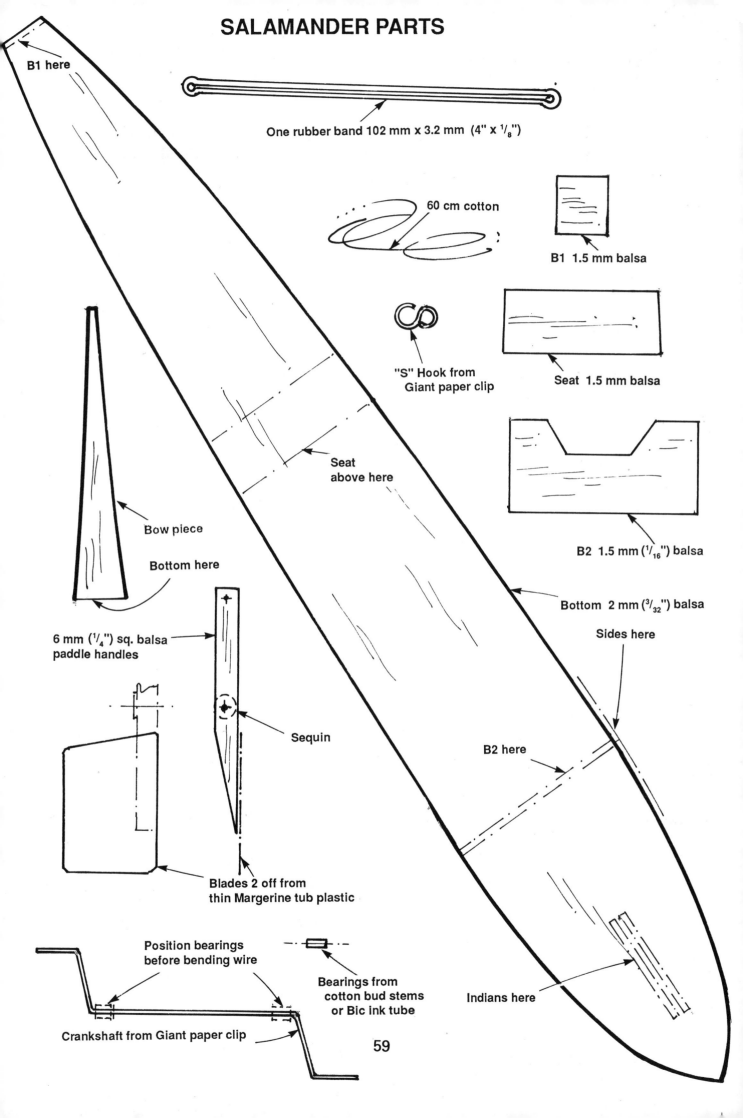

B1 here

One rubber band 102 mm x 3.2 mm (4" x $\frac{1}{8}$")

60 cm cotton

"S" Hook from Giant paper clip

B1 1.5 mm balsa

Seat 1.5 mm balsa

B2 1.5 mm ($\frac{1}{16}$") balsa

Bow piece

Bottom here

Seat above here

Bottom 2 mm ($\frac{3}{32}$") balsa

Sides here

B2 here

6 mm ($\frac{1}{4}$") sq. balsa paddle handles

Sequin

Blades 2 off from thin Margerine tub plastic

Position bearings before bending wire

Bearings from cotton bud stems or Bic ink tube

Indians here

Crankshaft from Giant paper clip

SALAMANDER ASSEMBLY

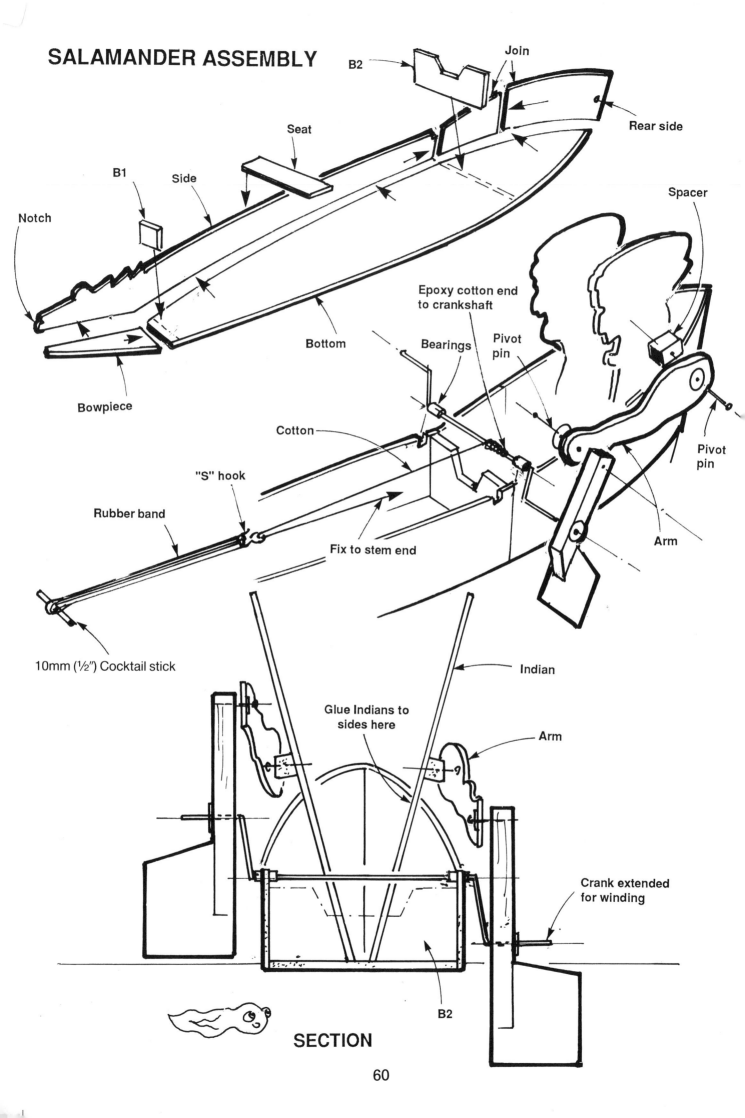

Join

B2

Rear side

Seat

Spacer

B1

Side

Notch

Epoxy cotton end
to crankshaft

Pivot
pin

Bearings

Bottom

Bowpiece

Cotton

Pivot
pin

"S" hook

Arm

Rubber band

Fix to stem end

10mm (½") Cocktail stick

Indian

Glue Indians to
sides here

Arm

Crank extended
for winding

B2

SECTION

60

PADDLE ACTION SEQUENCE

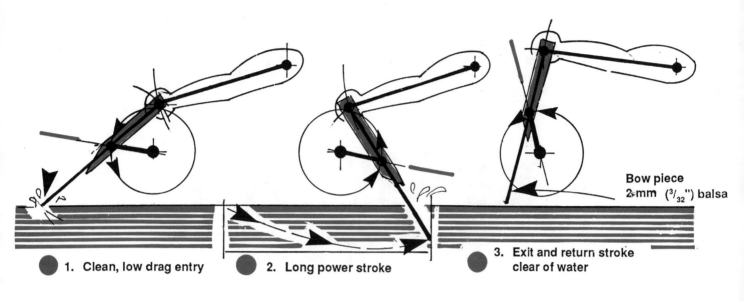

Bow piece
2-mm (³/₃₂") balsa

1. Clean, low drag entry

2. Long power stroke

3. Exit and return stroke clear of water

NOTE:
All the models described in this book have been built from the drawings and accompanying text, using only the recommended materials and assembly notes. The success of their operation will depend on the readers adherence to the instructions and his/her individual ability.

The sister volume to this book is also available. *Amazing Models! – Balloon Power* also contains instructions for making 12 models using the most basic materials but, in this case, the motive force comes from ordinary balloons.

Balloon Power costs £4.95 and can be obtained from any good bookshop or, in case of difficulty, direct from Argus Books.

Please add 50p for postage and packing.

ARGUS BOOKS
Mander Walsh, Milner Road
Chilton Industrial Estate
Sudbury, Suffolk

Subscribe now...

here's 3 good reasons why!

Within each issue these three informative magazines provide the expertise, and inspiration you need to keep abreast of developments in the exciting field of model aviation.

With regular new designs to build, practical features that take the mysteries out of construction, reports and detailed descriptions of the techniques and ideas of the pioneering aircraft modellers all over the world – they respresent three of the very best reasons for taking out a subscription. You need never miss a single issue or a single minute of aeromodelling pleasure again!

SUBSCRIPTION RATES

	U.K.	Europe	Middle East	Far East	Rest of World
RCM&E *Published monthly*	£18.00	£28.20	£28.90	£33.80	£31.90
Radio Modeller *Published monthly*	£18.00	£24.10	£24.50	£27.45	£26.30
Aeromodeller *Published monthly*	£23.40	£28.20	£28.40	£30.20	£28.70

Airmail Rates on Request

Your remittance with delivery details should be sent to:

The Subscriptions Manager **(CG1)**
Argus Specialist Publications
Argus House
Boundary Way
Hemel Hempstead
Herts
HP2 7ST